T0354376

No Wheat No Dairy No Problem

Delicious recipes for people with food allergies/sensitivity and everyone who is looking for healthy alternatives. The cookbook I wish I had!

BY

LAUREN HOOVER

iUniverse, Inc.
New York   Bloomington

iUniverse books may be ordered through booksellers or by contacting:

iUniverse
1663 Liberty Drive
Bloomington, IN 47403
www.iuniverse.com
1-800-Authors (1-800-288-4677)

Because of the dynamic nature of the Internet, any Web addresses or links contained in this book may have changed since publication and may no longer be valid. The views expressed in this work are solely those of the author and do not necessarily reflect the views of the publisher, and the publisher hereby disclaims any responsibility for them.

ISBN: 978-1-4401-4468-4 (sc)
ISBN: 978-1-4401-4469-1 (ebook)
ISBN: 978-1-4401-4470-7 (hc)

Library of Congress Control Number: 2009930712

Printed in the United States of America

iUniverse rev. date: 7/7/2009

Got Questions?

Need Answers?

Want to have a recipe converted?

Go to:

nowheatnodairynoproblem.com

Especially for You with Love

Disclaimer

It is not the intent of the author to diagnose, prescribe, treat or cure any medical condition. Nor is it the purpose of this book to replace the services of a health professional. It is advised to seek the advice of a licensed, professional healthcare provider for any condition that may require medical attention.

Contents

Introduction

Imagine waking up every day and going to sleep every night with a stomachache for most of your life! Somehow I knew that it couldn't be normal to wake up congested and have an ongoing stomachache, but nobody was coming up with any answers.

I was a pastry chef and was exposed to a lot of flour for a long time on a daily basis. I had heard that it was common for pastry chefs to develop wheat allergies due to overexposure. So, I suffered until I decided to eliminate wheat from my diet as a possible contributor to my ailments.

To my pleasant surprise I felt better after eliminating wheat altogether. My stomachaches were reduced, but they were still present and the congestion did not improve. Then, an Internist suggested that I eliminate dairy from my diet. At thirty-five years old, I was willing to try almost anything to feel better.

Well, it worked! After six weeks I woke up and realized that I could breathe and wasn't congested! This was the most amazing feeling I had for the first time. As for the stomachaches and permanent knot under my diaphragm, it disappeared too!

So, I went to the store to buy groceries, as I did every week, which was a pleasure until then. I couldn't believe how many products contained dairy and/or wheat including, cereal, bread, cookies, crackers, chips, soup, pasta, candy, prepared fresh/frozen foods etc... I left the store crying because I was sure I would starve or feel very deprived.

I cannot tell you how many wheat or dairy alternatives I have purchased and thrown away because they tasted terrible. This was so frustrating, not to mention expensive. Many alternatives are wheat free OR dairy free, but not both. I have only found a few cookbooks that are wheat or dairy free, but not both. The few cookbooks that I did find used unfamiliar or weird ingredients and refined sugar, which I do not want to eat. This cookbook does not use any refined sugar!

Having been a professional chef, I took this as a challenging opportunity to solve my problem. I wanted to eat all the things I had always enjoyed without wheat and dairy! So, off I went to my kitchen to try and convert traditional recipes into delicious alternatives for wheat and dairy free diets.

At this point in my life I had gone back to college to earn a Bachelors degree and was asking the question, and praying, "What is my purpose of being here in this lifetime and what can I give back to improve other people's lives"? A college friend of mine turned to me, after eating many of these recipes, and said, "Why don't you write a cookbook"!

And, this is how the cookbook came to be, and I found my purpose! I am thankful for the combination of food allergies and a culinary education so I can help as many people as possible.

My goal was to create dishes that tasted as good as or better than the traditional wheat and dairy recipes using healthy, familiar and easy to find ingredients. The main ingredients I have found as great substitutes include: Agave Nectar, Real Maple Syrup, Sucanat, Almond or Hazelnut Milk, Coconut Milk, Broth/Stock, Oat Flour, Olive Oil, Grapeseed Oil, Vegan Earth Balance and tapioca starch. I suggest alternatives if you are allergic or sensitive to these main ingredients too.

One recipe at a time I have compiled this book to satisfy my gourmet appetite without feeling deprived! I have always loved cooking and helping people so, what better gift to give to you than this cookbook. Even if you are not wheat or dairy intolerant/allergic, you will enjoy these healthy recipes that will provide variety in your diet.

Friends, family, colleagues, neighbors, and anyone else I could find, have been wonderful taste testers over the years and have loved these recipes-and never missed the wheat, dairy or refined sugar! So, don't cry when you walk past the ice cream store-just go home and make it yourself and enjoy! May this labor of love bring joy back into eating and cooking again or add variety to your culinary repertoire. I hope you will use this cookbook as a guide and it will help and inspire you to be creative in all of your cooking. Many blessings of health and happiness to you.

Acknowledgements

Thank you, Merci, Grazie, Gracias, Danka etc...

I offer my heartfelt gratitude to everyone who has helped me to create this cookbook and accomplish my life's purpose. There are so many people from perfect strangers to angels sent from heaven who have been an instrumental part of assisting me along this seven year project that I cannot mention everyone, but I am so thankful to each and every one of you.

However, there are a few very special Angels that I must declare my eternal gratitude for their love, support, encouragement and enormous generosity. First, this cookbook would not have ever existed or been completed without Divine guidance and never ending blessings which I am continually amazed and deeply thankful.

Mom, Dad and my little sister Mary Clo thank you for believing in me, encouraging me, and always being there for me which is so vital and valuable. For all the numerous things you have taught me and continue to teach me, I am so grateful. Mom, especially for introducing me to cooking at an early age and letting me stand on a wooden chair and help, where my passion for food began! For teaching me to make Béchamel sauce and many of the recipes in this cookbook that were inspired by you! For encouraging me to appreciate a variety of food from a very early age from Shrimp Cocktail, Fried Clams, Escargot, to many vegetables and mostly chocolate mousse!

My loving Great-Grandmother, Mimi, thank you for making me boiled chicken and a fried egg on toast and letting me eat it in bed watching Saturday morning cartoons! Shh, don't tell my Mother! And, for letting me eat honey out of the jar! Oh boy, I am really going to be in trouble when my Mother reads this!

My Grand Father who took me grocery shopping and gave me my first memory of food shopping, tasting and eating raw green beans and cooking asparagus in his pot that I still have today! For the fond memories of dipping toast in your coffee on the weekends!

Grand Father Artie, who was the Chef and partner at the Bella Vista in Woodside, California, who introduced me to so many delicious and exotic foods, like Frogs Legs-yours are still the best!

Eternal thanks, to Toti and Ernesto, my Angels, for opening your beautiful hearts and home to me. Allowing me to use your spectacular kitchen/kitchen accessories to test recipes and conduct the photo shoot, and the perfect white plates for the cover photos. Muchas Gracias Toti for giving me your office;

a peaceful and quiet space to write. And, for being my patient and honest taste testers! Ernesto and Rich, my personal IT support and brilliant engineers without your expertise this cookbook would never have been submitted-many heartfelt thanks. Misti and Lei, my new fury friends, for bringing fun, love, affection and humor into my life during this project. Looking forward to having some time in the hammock, for some much needed rest and a champagne toast to celebrate with you! Muchas Gracias!

Veronique, you have been such a good friend to me through all your loving kindness and encouragement. It is so helpful to have a friend who is a great cook and passionate about food to discuss ideas and cook together. I really appreciate all the articles, recipes, cookbooks/books, great meals made with love, enthusiastic encouragement, patient listening, music, laughter and rice bags! Thank you for lending me the beautiful English China for the cookbook cover/photo shoot, the only exception to plain white plates! This cookbook has more savory recipes, thanks to you-a brilliant idea! Merci Beaucoup! Thanks for introducing me to Celia at Omnivore Books in San Francisco where I will have my first cookbook reading/signing, and thank you Celia for having me!

Ronaldo, Mille Grazie per tutto! I always looked forward to spending weekends with you enjoying great food, fun, cooking and especially Saturday morning Pancakes! Thanks for tutoring me through college, always believing in me and how to make the best Margarita! And, thanks for doing the piles of dishes too! Nancy, thank you for listening and always knowing exactly what to say at the perfect moment, and all your gentle wisdom that comforts and encourages me. Thank you for sharing your Molasses Cake recipe with me too!

I am so grateful that iuniverse agreed to publish my cookbook. Everyone I have talked with at iuniverse has been so friendly and helpful, and provided an exceptionally high level of customer service. A special thanks to John Potts, Molly Weddle, Shawn Waggener, Thomas Gundry for your technical brilliance and for listening to me and guiding me through this process with such patience, kindness, humor and knowledge.

Many thanks to Allyson Wiley for taking the beautiful photographs for the cookbook! I really admire and appreciate your talent and unique style. Your keen eye knows just how to frame things to look their best!

Many thanks to all the wonderful people, dear friends along the way that have, and continue to, believe in me and are my cheerleaders-especially Cheri and Gene. To all the people who purchase this cookbook and share it with others, I thank you for assisting me in accomplishing my goal of helping as many people as possible including you! Many thanks, to all the culinary professionals who have taught me so much and have inspired me to continue to develop my own culinary skills and style. I wish all of you great success, with much health and joy. Bon Appétit!

Helpful Hints/Professional Secrets

Start with fresh, local and organic ingredients; they will be fresher and you will help reduce global warming and support local farmers too. Try to use fresh produce within one week. Cook and consume meat, poultry and fish within two days of purchase or freeze the same day.

Stay safe from food borne illness:

- Keep food below 40 degrees or above 140 degrees. Anything between is optimal for bacterial growth. Keep a thermometer in your refrigerator and keep it at 36-38 degrees

- Eat leftovers within 2-3 days or freeze

- Place labels on jars of food with date you opened it

- Defrost frozen food for 24 hours in the refrigerator instead of room temperature

- Put food away within one hour. The bacteria grows very rapidly, especially after the first hour. Keep cold food on ice when transporting it or at a buffet or party. Keep hot food above 140 degrees with heated serving trays or electric warmers.

- For a party that lasts longer than one

hour, put out food in small batches or pass appetizers instead of buffets-older children love this job!

- Wash your hands with soap before beginning to prepare food and after handling raw meat

- Teach your children to wash their hands just before eating

- Wash all utensils and cutting boards with hot water and soap, and put in dishwasher

- Use color coded cutting boards- blue for fish, red for meat, green for vegetables, orange for fruit

- Keep an oven thermometer in the oven as most ovens are off a little bit, and adjust dial as needed.

- Use an instant read thermometer to test meat for doneness by inserting it into the middle of the meat, away from the bone, where it will be the least done. Cook to listed temperature, cover with foil and rest covered at room temperature for 15 minutes to finish cooking and hold in the juices. Use current guidelines below:

  - Rare 125 degrees

  - Medium-rare 140 degrees

  - Well 160 degrees

  - Poultry 160 in thigh, 170 in breast

  - Fish cook until opaque white, and flaky

- Salmon until pink and fat is coming to surface, looks like white spots

Cooking secrets:

- Begin with a clean, uncluttered kitchen space

- Read the entire recipe first and follow it

- Get out all ingredients and utensils out before beginning to cook

- Clean as you go and you will have less of a mess later

- Keep all knives very sharp to avoid cuts and ease slicing/chopping!

- Invest in a good quality stainless steel chef knife and pots/pans like All Clad

- Clean pans with Bar Keepers Friend(an acid scrub)-use gloves

- Heat pans before adding oil. It is ready when food sizzles, and too hot if pan smokes

- Don't over crowd pans or fill more than ¾ of the way from the top, use large pots/pans

- Use timers. Don't rush, be patient and have fun!

- Make a weekly menu and shopping list to avoid throwing away food while saving time and money. "If you fail to plan, you plan to fail." Abraham Lincoln

- Taste food throughout the cooking process-you can always add more, but not take away

- Cook vegetables until just tender when toothpick is inserted, not mushy. If you like them with a little crunch, cook a minute or two less.

- For bright color, blanch vegetables in boiling water for 1 minute and directly into ice water for 1 minute, drain. Sauté in oil and season just before serving to finish cooking.

- Be adventurous and try new herbs and spices

- Throw away dried spices and herbs after 1 year for optimal flavor-buy small amounts

- Serve food as soon as it is finished cooking/ resting

- Warm plates in 170 degree oven for 5 minutes or in hot water or in microwave with a little water on the plates for 30 seconds to 1 minute

- Take a cooking class on the basic cooking methods and knife skills or at least buy a good cookbook with those instructions/ photos

Baking Secrets:

- Follow recipe exactly because baking has lots of chemistry (unless you are a chemist!)

- Buy new baking powder and baking soda and yeast once a year

- Preheat oven with an oven thermometer

- Bake on the middle rack unless recipes states otherwise

- Use a glass measuring cup for all wet/liquid ingredients

- Use metal or plastic measuring cups/spoons for all dry ingredients and level them off with the back of a knife

- Bake items with baking powder or baking soda immediately

- Begin checking if dessert is done 5 minutes before recipe says it will be done

- Always use a timer, but use your nose too!

- Cool baked items completely on racks to help air circulate around them before serving

- Use glass, ceramic baking dishes

- Use heavy professional baking cake pans and cookie sheets so they don't warp

- Grease cake pans with shortening and then dust with oat flour to avoid sticking

- Use a 2 ounce/1 Tablespoon size ice cream scooper with metal release to scoop cookie dough for uniformity

- Place cookie dough evenly spaced, three across and four down the cookie sheet

- Break eggs into a separate small bowl to be sure no shells end up in your food. To remove a broken eggshell, use the empty eggshell to scoop it out!

- See and read Main Ingredients page, Wheat Names, and Dairy Names pages

- Be sure to read labels on food, body and household cleaning products since our skin is our largest organ and absorbs what we put on it directly into the bloodstream! So, make sure your body care products do not contain wheat and/or dairy, which many do. I always use all natural products with no wheat, dairy, parabens or sodium laurel sulfates. I try to buy organic when they are available because I am assured they use the highest standards, controls and quality ingredients. This does not always mean they are more expensive. There are many small local people who make terrific products, you just need to find them-look at farmer's markets and small independent stores/boutiques or online.

Main Ingredients

Agave nectar: Tastes sweet and neutral. Extracted from the Blue Agave Cactus. Raw agave syrup has a low glycemic index and is absorbed into the body much slower than sugar. It eliminates the highs and lows experienced with eating refined sugar. Dissolves in cold liquid. Available in light and dark, use light unless recipe indicates dark.

Almond/Hazelnut Milk: High in Calcium! Water and almonds or hazelnuts blended together and used as a milk substitute. Unsweetened, Plain Rice Milk or Soy Milk can be used as a substitute if you are allergic to nuts. Buy organic, because they are heavily sprayed with pesticides.

Barley Flour: Whole Grain Flour made from ground Barley. Contains gluten. Can be used if allergic to Oats. Oat flour may be used instead.

Coconut milk: Coconut milk is the combination of coconut water and coconut oil. Light is available which has half the fat and calories of regular. Coconut water is very hydrating due to naturally occurring electrolytes, enzymes and vitamins; and is used in place of blood plasma in some countries. The water filters itself through the tree for nine months which makes it a sterile source of hydration. Coconut milk contains No Trans fat or cholesterol, and actually helps to balance cholesterol levels. Some sources recommend it be eaten in moderation, and others say it's abundant with healthy properties including breaking up accumulated fats in the system and metabolize them. This oil contains the highest amount of lauric acid next to mother's milk, which is anti-viral and anti-microbial! See website links for more information.

Coconut oil: Coconut oil is a raw saturated fat containing mostly medium-chain fatty acids, which the body can metabolize efficiently and convert to energy quickly. The refined coconut oil has a more neutral flavor than the unrefined which has a distinctive coconut flavor. See website links for more information.

Date Sugar: finely ground dried date crystals. Can be used in place of sugar. Very expensive.

Grapeseed oil: oil extracted from grape seeds. Very high in antioxidants and can tolerate very high heat. Has a neutral flavor. Can be interchanged with safflower or sunflower oil.

Maple Syrup: syrup/sap from the Sugar Maple Tree

that is boiled and evaporated. A flavorful sweetener. Also dried and made into crystals, known as Maple Sugar.

Molasses: use unsulfured. Cane sugar syrup, unrefined/unprocessed. Great in gingerbread/snaps.

Oat Flour: ground rolled oats. High in fiber. Many people with celiac disease and on gluten free diets can tolerate oats. Aids in reducing bad cholesterol. Barley flour may be substituted if allergic to oats.

Olive Oil: oil extracted from olives. Use extra virgin, cold-pressed for best quality. Extra virgin should not be heated over 350 degrees. Try the citrus olive oils for additional flavor.

Stock/Broth: vegetable, chicken, beef or seafood may be used as a liquid in recipes in place of milk or cream. Adds more flavor than plain water in recipes and rice.

Sucanat: dehydrated, unprocessed sugar cane juice. Fine ground golden brown crystals. An affordable, raw sweetener with a light molasses flavor. Interchangeable with maple/date sugar.

Tapioca Starch: ground tapioca. Used to thicken sauces and puddings. Similar and interchangeable with arrowroot and/or cornstarch. Less allergenic than cornstarch.

Vegan Earth Balance: a vegetable spread/sticks made without any hydrogenated or Trans fats.

Almond Milk/Hazelnut Milk

2 ½ cups raw organic almonds or hazelnuts

6 cups filtered water

1 tsp. real vanilla extract, optional

agave nectar, optional

If you are using almonds, place them in a glass or plastic container and cover with filtered water and refrigerate for 12 hours to make them more digestible. Drain and rinse. Hazelnuts do not need to be soaked because they do not have an enzyme inhibitor.

Place nuts and filtered water into blender. Pulse on low until the water turns white, and nuts are small chunks. If you over mix the nuts and they are too fine, the milk will not be smooth.

Add 1 tsp. vanilla extract and agave nectar to taste if desired. Drain through fine strainer or cheesecloth and squeeze out extra liquid. Save nuts for hummus or sprinkle on cereal or salad.

The milk will keep in the refrigerator for 1 week. Place a sticker with a best before date on the container. I like to keep it in a glass pitcher or glass mason jar. You can freeze it- just shake it as it may separate when defrosted.

Use in place of milk in any recipe, eat with cereal or make a smoothie by adding fruit!

Oat Flour

2-4 cups organic rolled oats

You can do this in batches. Either use a blender, food processor with the S blade or a vitamixer. Add the oats, hold the cover on and blend until fine. You may need to scrape the oats down if they stick to the side-be sure to do this with the machine off. Now, you have oat flour! Easy and fast!

The vitamixer grinds the oats the finest.

Bread

Cornbread

This is wonderful served warm with honey spread! It goes very well with chili too. Makes a great stuffing for Turkey or anything you want to stuff.

Yields: 1 (8x8) pan

¾ cup oat flour

¼ cup millet flour

1 cup cornmeal, fine to medium grind

1 teaspoon baking powder

½ teaspoon baking soda

½ teaspoon sea salt, fine

¼ cup whole millet, optional

1 cup almond milk

1 lg. egg, organic

¼ cup grapeseed oil or corn oil

¼ cup honey (clover, orange)

Honey spread (see Index)

Sift flours, baking powder, baking soda and salt into the mixing bowl of an electric stand mixer or bowl, add the remaining dry ingredients and mix. Add the wet ingredients and mix just until combine. Scrape sides and bottom of the bowl.

Grease an 8x8 glass baking dish with vegan Earth Balance. Pour batter into pan and let it sit for 15 minutes to let grains absorb the liquid. Preheat oven to 425 degrees. Bake on the middle rack of the oven for 20 minutes or until toothpick comes out clean from the center. Cool in the pan for 10 minutes, cut and serve. May be reheated in the oven for 5 minutes or microwave for 10-30 seconds depending on the size of the piece!

Irish Soda Bread

This bread is very quick to make-no rising necessary. The outside is a little crunchy with a moist cakey biscuit texture. Add whatever dried fruit, nuts or spices you like. This will transport you to the green grassy hills in the countryside of Ireland!

Yields: 1 (8 inch) round loaf

2 cups oat flour

2 cups barley or soy flour

1 Tablespoon baking powder

2 teaspoons baking soda

1 teaspoon sea salt, fine

1 cup almond milk*

3 Tablespoons grapeseed oil or extra virgin olive oil

2 lg. organic eggs, beaten

2 Tablespoons agave nectar

1 Tablespoon lemon or orange zest, optional

½ cup of raisins or any diced dried fruit (apricots, pears, cherries etc...), optional

½ cup chopped nuts (walnuts, pecans), optional

1 teaspoon caraway seeds or fennel seeds or poppy seeds, optional

Preheat oven to 375 degrees

Butter and flour an 8 inch round cake pan, set aside. In an electric stand mixer, sift all dry ingredients into the mixing bowl. Add all the wet ingredients, zest, dried fruit and spices/seeds. Using a paddle attachment, mix on low speed just until flour is combined. Using a rubber spatula scrape the sides and bottom of the bowl to be sure it is evenly mixed. Pour batter into 8 inch round cake pan and smooth with spatula so it is higher in the center. Bake immediately on the middle rack of the oven for 40 minutes, or until a knife comes out clean. The color will be a dark brown. Cool for at least 15 minutes and remove from pan onto a cooling rack. Serve warm or room temperature. I like it best warm with a little vegan Earth Balance and fruit spread or lemon curd for breakfast or with afternoon tea. However, it is also good with dinner as savory bread especially with the seeds and no fruit. Also good with Honey Spread (see index).

* Substitute for soy milk or rice milk if allergic to nuts

Spelt Bread

This is the only flour I have had success with making bread so far, keep an eye on my blog site and the next cookbook for more….need to keep testing. This bread is very similar to a traditional Country Wheat Bread baked in a bakery. It has a crunchy crust and is chewy and soft inside. Not everyone with a wheat sensitivity/allergy can tolerate Spelt, but many of us can! This is not wheat or gluten free. Spelt is one of the 5 ancient grains of Israel and is in the wheat family.

Note: This takes 7 hours to prepare and another 2-10 for the poolish to ferment-it's an all day project that begins the night before. Plan ahead.

Yields: 2 round 10 inch loaves

Poolish:

½ cup bottled or filtered water (75 degrees)

½ teaspoon dry yeast (not quick rising)

¾ cup spelt flour

Final Dough:

2 ½ cups bottled or filtered water

½ teaspoon dry yeast

6 cups spelt flour

1 Tablespoon sea salt, fine

Optional additions:

2 cups chopped walnuts, optional

1 Tablespoon fresh rosemary chopped, optional

2 cups raisins or diced dried fruit (apricots, pears), optional

Be sure to check the date on the yeast to see that it is still good or it will not work. Heat water in microwave or in a pot on the stove. Use a thermometer to check for exact temperature of the water, this is very important.

In a small bowl, stir together warm water and yeast. Let it sit for a minute or two to dissolve and then stir together. Stir in flour until it is the consistency of thick batter. With a wooden spoon stir the poolish 100 times to develop the gluten. If you are in a hurry: Cover with plastic wrap and put in a warm (75-80 degrees) draft free place until mixture is bubbly grown in volume. If my house is too cold, I will put a cup of water in the microwave oven and heat it for 1 minute then place the bowl of polish into the microwave with the cup of water next to it. If you can, start the night before: omit setting it out at room temperature and just cover with plastic wrap and refrigerate overnight or up to 10 hours. Remove from refrigerator. The poolish should be bubbly and grown in volume. Measure out all ingredients for the final dough. With a silicone spatula, scrape dough into a large metal bowl. Add the water, yeast and salt to the poolish and stir until combined. Add one cup of flour at a time until the dough is very difficult to stir. Put dough on top of a well floured board. Dust your hands with flour since the dough will be sticky at first and will get smoother as it is kneaded. Knead the dough by pushing the heel of your hand forward on the dough and then pulling back from the top and folding the dough over with the other hand. Continue to turn the dough one quarter turn each time you fold. Keep folding and kneading for 15 minutes-yes, this is a great workout. If the dough is still wet and sticky, add more flour. It will become more elastic as you knead. It can be slightly tacky, but not so sticky it is sticking to everything. To test if it is kneaded enough press your finger into the dough and if it springs back, it's ready!

Yes, a heavy duty electric mixer can be used, but I do not recommend it as I stripped the gears of mine by making bread. It is more fun to make it by hand and the texture seems to be better. If you must use an electric stand mixer, mix the dough with a dough hook for about 12 minutes on medium speed-do not use high speed. If the dough springs back it's done. If not, add a little more flour and knead 3-5 minutes more or finish kneading by hand to get a more accurate idea of when it is done. Make sure the mixer is far away from the edge of the counter as it may move during mixing.

Shape the dough into a ball. Put 2 teaspoons of extra

virgin olive oil a large metal bowl, add the dough and turn it over to coat the outside with oil. Cover and put in a warm place (75-80 degrees) to rise for 2-3 hours or until double in volume. The microwave oven is a good place, see my note above. When you push your finger into the dough it should leave an indentation when it is ready.

Deflate the dough by pushing down on the center and pulling up the sides. Form in a ball, cover and rest for 30 more minutes. Deflate the dough and cut in half and shape both balls of dough into tight balls by kneading. Place on top of a baking sheet with space in between the balls as they will increase in volume. Cover with a clean damp towel or plastic wrap and put into a warm, draft free place about 78 degrees for 1 ½ to 2 hours or until increased in volume by 1 ½ times.

Thirty minutes before baking, preheat the oven to 450 degrees with the rack in the middle of the oven. Fill a clean spray bottle with filtered or bottled water and spray the sides and bottom of the oven until steam forms just before baking the dough. BE CAREFUL, not to spray the light bulb or it will shatter. Place bread in oven. Close the door and bake 3 minutes and spray again and bake for 20 minutes. Turn the oven down to 400 degrees and bake until loaves are dark brown and crust is firm about 15-20 more minutes. To test the doneness, turn the loaves over and firmly tap on the bottom and it's done when it sounds hollow like a drum. If not, bake another 5 minutes and test again. Remove from oven and cool on a rack at least 20 minutes which will finish the baking process. If you skip this cooling period the dough will be doughy and uncooked in the center. Be sure to put them on a rack so they can have air circulating around the entire loaf. If they are sitting on a surface the bottom will get soggy. When completely cool, slice on a wooden board with a serrated knife and spread with vegan Earth Balance or dip in extra virgin olive oil. This is so delicious that it is worth waiting every minute to enjoy! Makes great garlic bread and croutons for Caesar salad or to top soup! Ah, it makes great sandwiches when sliced thin. Put any hard leftover cubed bread into a blender or food processor to make bread crumbs.

Storage: will keep at room temperature, cut side down on a board for 3 days. Best kept at room temperature uncovered so the crust will stay crispy. The whole loaf may be frozen if wrapped well in plastic and put into a freezer zip bag. Once thawed, bake at 350 degrees for 10 minutes to crisp it up.

Main Dishes

Bourguignon

Everything is better with red wine! The benefit of braising is very tender meat and a rich sauce to spoon over mashed potatoes or dip with spelt bread. This is a great chance to try a new meat!

Yields: 6-8 servings

3 Tablespoons grapeseed oil

2 pounds buffalo or venison or beef, 1½ inch cubes*

1 pound crimini mushrooms, washed and quartered

½ cup dry sherry

¼ cup ruby port

2 Tablespoons tomato paste

4 cups red wine* (Burgundy, Zinfandel, Pinot Noir)

2 cups beef stock

1 pound frozen pearl onions

1 bay leaf

3 sprigs fresh thyme

Sea salt/freshly ground black pepper, to taste

¼ cup oat or potato flour mixed with ½ cup cold water (shake in a glass jar)

In a large Dutch oven or stainless steel soup pot with a lid over high heat sauté meat in 2 Tablespoons oil until brown on both sides, set aside. In the same pot, sauté mushrooms in 1 Tablespoon of oil until tender. Return meat to pot. Deglaze pan with sherry and port, cook until reduced by half. Stir in the remaining ingredients. Bring to a boil over high heat. Stir in flour/water mixture and cook for 2 minutes while stirring. Preheat oven to 350 degrees. Cover Dutch oven and bake on the middle rack of the oven for approximately 1 ½ hours or until meat is very tender. Remove from oven and pull out stems of thyme and bay leaf. Salt and pepper to taste. Serve immediately. Excellent with mashed potatoes (see index).

*I recommend buying organic or "no sulfites added" wine. Organic wine has significantly less sulfites than traditional wines. Many people are sensitive to sulfites and may not be aware of it.

*See Resources to find sources for buffalo or venison. Available online and at Whole Foods Market. Butchers at your grocery store may be able to special order it.

Chicken Pot Pie

Chicken Pot Pie is one of the most comforting foods. To save time make ahead and freeze, then bake frozen pie. This recipe takes a total of 2 ½ hours from start to finish, but is well worth it.

Yields: 1 pie

1 whole organic free range chicken, cooked or 4 boneless chicken breasts or thighs cubed

1 small organic yellow onion, diced small

2 cloves fresh garlic, chopped finely

1 cup sliced organic carrots

4 stalks organic celery, sliced

½ cup organic frozen petite green peas

1 bunch organic flat Italian parsley, finely chopped

1 teaspoon dried basil

1 teaspoon dried thyme or 2 teaspoon fresh thyme

1 teaspoon dried tarragon or 2 teaspoons fresh tarragon

1 teaspoon dried marjoram or dried savory or ½ teaspoon dried oregano

1 bay leaf

4 Tbsp. organic oat flour

4 Tbsp. organic grapeseed oil or extra virgin olive
oil

1 cup organic or free-range chicken stock or 1
organic bouillon cube +1 cup hot water

sea salt/pepper to taste

1 recipe of pie crust, unbaked and chilled

Make pie crust and refrigerate-great to do this ahead to save you time. You can either use raw chicken pieces or leftover chicken or a whole precooked chicken, which is a great time saver! Roll out half the pie dough, in between plastic wrap or on a well floured board, to ¼ inch thick and about 1 inch wider than your pie pan. Roll dough around rolling pin and unroll over a glass pie dish, refrigerate for 20 minutes-you can omit this layer of crust for less calories. Keep the other half of dough refrigerated. Wash and chop all the vegetables on a clean cutting board, set aside. On clean cutting board cut raw chicken into 1 inch cubes, set aside. If using cooked chicken, remove and cut up breasts and thighs into 1 inch cubes and remove skin and bones. Wash everything that the chicken touched with hot water/soap to kill all the bacteria that can cause food borne illness. Preheat oven to 375 degrees. In a large pot sauté 4 Tablespoons oil, raw chicken, onion, carrots and celery over medium high heat until vegetables are soft, and chicken is browned. If using cooked chicken do not add it until later.

In the same pot add flour and whisk over medium high heat for 2 minutes. Slowly add the chicken stock while whisking vigorously to avoid lumps. Bring to a boil and add frozen green peas, herbs and chopped parsley, cook 2 minutes. Season mixture with pepper and salt if needed and remove bay leaf. Add cooked chicken at this point. Mix everything together and pour into pie pan lined with dough. Roll out remaining half of dough about 1 inch wider than pie pan, cut a ½ inch hole in the middle and place over the top of the pie, and crimp the edges with your thumb and fingers or a fork. Bake at 375 degrees on top of a baking sheet on the middle rack of the oven for 1 hour or until it is bubbling in the middle and the crust is golden brown. Remove from oven; let it cool for 5-10 minutes. Cut into slices, serve and enjoy. This will keep in the refrigerator for a few days.

Chili

This is very warming on a cold day. You can make this very flavorful and spicy dish with turkey, chicken, buffalo, venison or beef. I like it with ground turkey, buffalo or venison. Using ground meat will cut the cooking time down, so it's great if you are in a hurry. Delicious served with cornbread (see index). Top the chili with diced raw onion and chopped cilantro. Be creative!

Yields: serves 4

2 pounds ground turkey or ground buffalo or meat, cut into 1 inch cubes

2 Tablespoons grapeseed oil

1 large onion, diced

4 cloves garlic, pressed or minced

1 cup chili powder

1 teaspoon ancho chili powder

2 Tablespoon ground cumin

2 Tablespoon dried oregano or 4 Tablespoons fresh oregano

¼-1 teaspoon cayenne pepper (mild to very hot)

1 cinnamon stick

1 ½ cups good bottled beer (pale ale is excellent)-the cook can drink the rest!

4 cups chicken or beef stock or broth

1 14 ounce can kidney beans or white beans, optional

1 14 ounce can organic diced tomatoes, unsalted if possible

½ cup oat flour mixed with ½ cup cold water

Sea salt and freshly ground black pepper, to taste

In a large soup pot, sauté meat over high heat until brown or ground meat is cooked, set aside. Add onion and garlic over medium high heat until golden brown. Add spices and stir to combine. Pour in beer, stock, beans and tomatoes. Add meat. Bring to a boil, stir and reduce heat to low. Cover and simmer over low heat for 30 minutes for ground meat and 1 hour for chunks of meat. In a glass jar, make slurry with oat flour and water, cover and shake until flour is dissolved. Uncover chili, stir in flour slurry. Cover and cook over low heat for 30 minutes or until meat is tender. Serve. Great with cornbread (see index).

Crab Cakes

This takes me back to the crab shacks along the Atlantic seashore, and I can almost smell the ocean and feel the warm breeze on my face when I eat them! Keeping them simple is the secret.

Yields: approximately 12 cakes

3 Tablespoons organic mayonnaise, no preservatives please

1 lg. organic egg

1 Tablespoon Worcestershire sauce

1 teaspoon Bay seasoning

¼ teaspoon freshly ground black pepper

1 teaspoon honey

1 teaspoon Dijon mustard, no preservatives please

1 teaspoon Tabasco or hot sauce

zest and juice of 1 washed lemon

1/3 cup flat leaf parsley, chopped

1 pound lump crabmeat, cleaned

3 slices spelt or rice bread, ½ inch dice or 3 cups cubed cornbread

Peanut oil or vegetable oil-for frying, about 2 cups or to fill halfway up frying pan*

2 lemons, washed and cut into 6 wedges each

In a large bowl, combine all wet ingredients, except egg and peanut oil, and whisk until smooth. Taste and adjust seasoning to your taste. Whisk in egg. Add parsley, crabmeat and bread, stir gently by folding with a wooden spoon from the middle to the edges. Cover and refrigerate for 1 hour. Make 12 equal sized round patties about 4 inches wide and ¾ inch thick-can use a measuring cup for this or a large ice cream scooper. Place on a baking sheet and set next to the frying pan. Pour oil into a cast iron frying pan or a deep frying pan with a thick bottom. Attach a thermometer to the side of the pan with the end just above the bottom. Heat the oil to 360 degrees over high heat. Using a spatula, gently slide four of them into the hot oil. Be careful, it will splatter. Adjust heat to keep oil at 350 degrees. Cook 3-4 minutes on each side until brown, but not burned. Turn only once by using a spatula underneath and a large spoon on the top of the cake and gently turn it over. Drain on a baking sheet lined with paper towels. Keep the baking sheet in the oven on the lowest temperature to keep them warm. *Can be baked at 375 for approximately 30 minutes instead of frying, but will not be as crispy. Serve immediately with a wedge of lemon. A green salad and a glass of white wine or champagne is a very nice compliment to these delicious crab cakes! Also good over a Caesar Salad (see index). Refrigerate any leftovers and reheat in a 375 degree oven for 10 minutes or until hot.

"Creamed" Tuna

This is a childhood favorite and true comfort food. It's also great when my refrigerator is bare!

Yields: 2-4 servings

1 recipe of "cream" sauce (see index)-using chicken stock

1 can tuna in water

½ cup frozen petite green peas

fresh dill or parsley, chopped, optional

1 cup cooked rice (jasmine, basmati or brown)

Make "cream" sauce and add tuna, with water in the can, and peas. Heat over medium heat just until it comes to a boil. Serve over cooked rice. Garnish with fresh chopped dill or parsley.

Curry

This yellow curry will transport you to India, without a long plane ride or jet lag! Coconut milk is cooling and the spices and chilies are warming along with sweet and salty condiments-a perfect balance. Serve over coconut rice (see index) with lots of condiments. Every year my mother would make this for my birthday dinner; and it was a special treat. Now, I make it for dinner parties and everyone loves it!

Yields: 4 servings

1 recipe of coconut rice (see index)

4 Tablespoons grapeseed oil

1 pound boneless, skinless chicken breast or thigh, or 1 pound raw peeled jumbo shrimp

1 medium onion, diced

2 cloves garlic, minced

1 Tablespoon ginger root, minced

2 organic green apples, cored and diced

2 Tablespoons ground coriander

2 teaspoons ground cumin

¼ teaspoon cayenne pepper, optional

½ teaspoon ground turmeric

¼ teaspoon ground cinnamon

1/8 teaspoon ground cloves

1 teaspoon ground fennel

¼ teaspoon fenugreek

4 curry leaves, optional

¾ cup regular coconut milk

½ cup chicken or fish stock

1 jalapeno pepper or 1 small Thai red pepper, seeded and minced

1 14 ounce can diced organic tomatoes, drained

Condiments: all are optional, add or remove any that you wish

Mango chutney

Tamarind chutney

1 large organic tomato or 2 Roma tomatoes, diced

2 hard boiled eggs, diced

1 bunch scallions, sliced

½ cup raisins

½ cup chopped peanuts

½ cup shredded unsweetened and toasted coconut

1 cup sliced fresh kumquats, seeded

2 sliced organic bananas (slice just before serving to retain color)

4 slices cooked bacon, crumbled

1 bunch cilantro, chopped

In a large soup pot or skillet, sauté the chicken in oil until brown, over medium high heat remove and set aside. If using shrimp, add it 2 minutes before serving and only cook for 2-3 minutes for tender shrimp. If you cook them too long they will be very tough. In the same pan, sauté onions, garlic and ginger until translucent. Add apples, jalapeno and all spices and sauté over medium heat for 2 minutes. Add chicken then pour in stock, coconut milk and tomatoes, stir. Bring to a boil and then lower heat to low; cover and simmer for 20 minutes, stirring occasionally. In the meantime, chop and prepare the condiments and put them in separate white ramekins or small glass bowls and put small spoons in each condiment bowl. Place them all on a Lazy Susan, rotating round tray, or any tray. Place this in the middle of the dining room table or on the buffet where people can help themselves. This can be done ahead of time. The chicken curry can also be cooked ahead of time and reheated over the stove in the oven or microwave. Do not reheat the shrimp, they need to be cooked and eaten immediately. Either put hot cooked coconut rice in a large serving bowl or a serving in the middle of each dinner plate. Spoon the curry over the rice or serve in a large bowl with a ladle. Tell everyone what the condiments are and invite them to sprinkle a little of everything on top of the curry and enjoy. This is a lot of work, but it is well worth it and you will be a star with everyone who enjoys it! Note: If you don't have the spices, you can add 3 Tablespoons of prepared curry powder, but it is really worth making it yourself. I recommend buying the spices in small quantities in the bulk section of your grocery store or going to an Indian market and buying them in bulk and sharing them with friends. You can make a large batch of the curry spices and bottle it as a gift along with this recipe, or their own copy of this cookbook, for your guests to take home. Thank you for sharing this cookbook!

Fried Chicken

A Southern favorite, hot or cold and great for picnics or anytime for that matter. I remember being so excited when I would find this nice surprise in my brown bag lunch at school! Wonderful served with mashed potatoes or potato salad and coleslaw.

Yields: 1 chicken, serves 4

brine (see index)

1 whole organic, free-range chicken cut up

unsweetened almond milk

hot sauce (Tabasco)

4 Tablespoons poultry seasoning

kosher salt for seasoning

½ teaspoon freshly ground black pepper

4 cups oat or barley or rice flour (oat is best)

2 cups grapeseed or peanut oil

Cut chicken breasts in half from side to side to speed cooking time. Prepare brine as directed. Soak chicken in brine from 2-48 hours in the refrigerator. If you are in a hurry, you can skip the brine, but it will not be as flavorful, tender and moist. Pour oil into a cast iron frying pan or heavy bottom sauté pan and place a thermometer on the side of the pan with the end just above the bottom of the pan. Heat oil over medium heat to 350 degrees. While oil is heating up, pour almond milk and hot sauce into a large bowl or 9x13 glass baking dish. In a plastic zip bag or a 9x13 baking dish combine the kosher salt, black pepper, poultry seasoning and oat flour and shake or whisk to combine. Transfer chicken from brine into the flour and coat it, shaking off excess flour. Dip into almond milk/hot sauce mixture and then back into the flour. Shake off excess flour. Gently lower into 350 degree oil skin side down. Cook for 12 minutes keeping temperature at 350 by adjusting the heat as necessary. Turn the chicken over with metal tongs and cook for another 10 minutes or until the internal temperature is at 165 degrees. When checking the internal temperature, insert thermometer into the thickest part in the middle of the breast or thigh, away from the bone (which is hotter). Remove from pan and drain on a rack over a baking sheet or lined with paper towels. Serve immediately or chill for later.

Fried Fish Filets

I have fond memories of going out to lunch with my Great Grandmother for fish and chips. She was so cute with her little white gloves; that I am surprised she would eat such a thing! I don't remember, but I bet she used a fork and knife! I dedicate this recipe to her in very loving memory.

Yields: 4-8 servings

2 cups grapeseed oil or vegetable shortening

4-8 (4 ounce) fish filets ¾ inch thick, such as cod or flounder

1 ¾ cup water or good bottled beer

2 cups oat or rice flour

¼ teaspoon baking soda

½ teaspoon sea salt, fine

First, I suggest you turn on the oven's exhaust fan on high and open the windows to prevent your house from smelling like oily fish. Pour oil or shortening into a 10 inch cast iron or sauté pan and place a thermometer on the side of the pan so the end is just above the bottom of the pan. Heat oil or shortening over medium high heat until it reaches 350 degrees. While oil is heating, whisk all ingredients except fish in a large bowl until smooth. Wash and dry the fish. Season the fish with salt and freshly ground pepper.

You can cut the fish filets into 1 inch strips if you like or leave them whole. Dip fish into batter to coat it on all sides completely. Immediately and very gently lower them into the oil. Do not crowd the pan-the fish should not be touching each other so they will cook evenly. Cook the fish in batches if necessary and keep the cooked fish in the oven on warm or the lowest setting on a baking sheet. Cover the pan with a frying screen to reduce the oil from splattering all over your kitchen. Fry on one side for 2 minutes for small pieces and 3 minutes for the whole filet. With a slotted fish spatula and another slotted spatula or large metal fork, gently roll the fish over onto the other side. Cook for 2-3 more minutes until golden brown. While fish is cooking line a baking sheet with paper towels and set next to the frying pan. Drain fish on the paper towel lined baking sheet. Serve immediately. Serve with wedges of washed cut lemon wedges and malt vinegar and or homemade tartar sauce. Great with French fries (see index) or roasted potatoes (see index).

Meatloaf

Great served hot with mashed potatoes or served cold for lunch! Use leftovers for tacos too!

Yields: 2 loaf pans, serves 8

1 yellow or white onion, sautéed

2 pounds ground meat (turkey*, chicken, buffalo, lamb or beef)

¾ cup organic ketchup

2 Tablespoons Worcestershire sauce

2 teaspoons hot sauce

½ bunch flat leaf parsley, chopped finely

2 teaspoons dried herbs or 1 Tablespoon fresh herbs, chopped (basil, thyme, savory, marjoram)

1 lg. organic egg

½ cup organic ketchup for topping, optional

Preheat oven to 375 degrees. Sauté onion and oil in a large sauté pan over medium heat until translucent and beginning to brown, set aside to cool off of the heat. Put turkey into a large glass or metal bowl, set aside. Measure all liquid ingredients into a glass measuring cup with herbs/parsley and whisk until well combined and pour over turkey meat. Add onion to turkey meat and mix everything together with very clean hands until well combined. If you can't stand to touch raw meat, this can be mixed in an electric stand mixer with the paddle attachment on low speed! Be sure to wash everything with hot water and soap that has come in contact with raw meat to prevent foodborne illness. Divide the turkey meat in half and put into 2 loaf pans. If you like, spread ¼ cup ketchup evenly over the top of each meatloaf with a spoon or spatula. Bake meatloaves on the middle rack of the oven for 1 hour or until internal temperature is 160 degrees. Remove from oven and carefully drain off any liquid. Run hot water with soap down the drain to avoid any clogs from grease! You didn't know you were going to get plumbing tips from this book did you?! Cool meatloaves for 5 minutes and serve immediately. If you have any leftover, let it cool for 1 hour at room temperature, cover and refrigerate. As a child, I loved meatloaf sandwiches in my sack lunch! As an adult, I use leftovers for tacos so I don't have to eat the same thing for days! Yum!

*I recommend turkey since it is lower in fat than red meat. Try a different kind of meat each time for variety! Be sure to use meat that has some fat so it will not be dry...don't buy the all white/breast meat or lean ground meat for this recipe.

Moussaka

A traditional baked Greek dish with lamb, eggplant and vegetables in custard. Moussaka is a comforting, hearty main dish with the texture of ground lamb and creamy custard. The Greek Gods must have thought they were in Heaven!

Yields: 9x9 dish, serves 6

2 Tablespoons grapeseed oil

2 Tablespoons extra virgin olive oil

1 pound ground lamb

½ white or yellow onion

2 cloves garlic, crushed

¼ cup brandy

½ cup diced canned tomatoes, drained

½ cup shredded carrots

1 Tablespoon ground cumin

1 teaspoon dried tarragon

½ teaspoon dried oregano

1 ½ teaspoons marjoram

¼ teaspoon ground cinnamon

1 teaspoon sea salt, fine

½ teaspoon freshly ground black pepper

2 Tablespoons extra virgin olive oil

½ pound crimini mushrooms, sliced

1 Tablespoon extra virgin olive oil or olive oil spray (for eggplant)

1 large eggplant, ¼ inch slices horizontally

sea salt for sprinkling over eggplant.

Custard:

5 lg. organic eggs

1 cup regular coconut milk

½ teaspoon sea salt, fine

¼ teaspoon freshly ground black pepper

¼ teaspoon freshly grated nutmeg

To prevent bitterness lay eggplant on a baking sheet and sprinkle with sea salt. Let them sit for 30 minutes or until water has come to the top, and dry with paper towels. In a 10-12 inch pot, over medium high heat, sauté the onions and garlic in grapeseed and olive oil until translucent. Add ground lamb to onions and cook until brown and well done. Set aside. Over high heat, sauté mushrooms in olive oil until tender. Add meat to mushrooms. Pour in brandy and cook over high heat until almost evaporated. Stir in all other ingredients except eggplant, olive oil and custard. Take meat off the heat and set aside. Either brush eggplant with 1 Tablespoon olive oil on both sides or lightly spray with olive oil spray and put on a baking sheet. Turn on oven to Broil. Put eggplant on the top shelf and broil for 4 minutes on one side, turn eggplant over with a spatula and broil 4 more minutes. Remove from oven and set aside. Turn down oven to 350 degrees. Whisk all custard ingredients together in a large bowl. Pour half custard mixture into meat and stir. Put a pot of water on to boil for baking dish. In a 9x9 glass baking dish place one half of the eggplant in a single layer. With a rubber or silicone spatula, evenly spread half meat mixture over the eggplant. Lay remaining eggplant over meat in a single layer. With a rubber or silicone spatula, evenly spread remaining meat over eggplant. Pour remaining custard over the top of the meat. Put baking dish into a larger baking dish and place on the center rack of the oven with the rack pulled out ¼ of the way. Carefully pour the boiling water into the outer baking dish until it is halfway up the Moussaka dish, being careful not to pour any into the Moussaka. This will prevent the custard from curdling/scrambling. The French call it a Bain Marie, or water bath. Bake for 55 minutes or until the custard is set and no liquid is at the top. Cool for 5 minutes, cut and serve with sautéed greens (see index) or a green salad with red wine vinaigrette (see index).

Mushroom Pot Pie

This is a great vegetarian main dish! The Portobello mushrooms have a meat like texture!

Yields: 1 pie, 6-8 servings

1 small organic yellow onion, diced

1 cup sliced organic carrots

4 stalks organic celery, sliced

2 large Portobello mushrooms, cubed or 4 cups crimini mushroom caps, halved

1/3 cup dry sherry, optional

1 cup organic frozen petite green peas

1 bunch organic flat Italian parsley, chopped

4 Tablespoons organic oat flour

4 Tablespoons organic grapeseed oil or extra virgin olive oil

2 cups organic vegetable stock or broth

salt/pepper to taste

2 teaspoons dried herbs (thyme, basil, savory, marjoram or your favorite)

1 recipe of pie crust, unbaked (see index)

Preheat oven to 375 degrees. Roll out half the pie dough to ¼ inch thick and about 1 inch wider than your pie pan, place in pie pan, refrigerate for 30 minutes or more. Keep the other half of dough refrigerated.

In a large pot saute onion, carrots celery and mushrooms over medium high heat until soft. Add ¼ cup dry sherry and cook for 1 minute until liquid has cooked down*, set aside. In the same pot add oil and flour and whisk over medium high heat until bubbling and then cook an additional 2 minutes. Slowly add the vegetable stock while whisking vigorously to avoid lumps. Bring to a boil and add all of the mushrooms, vegetables, frozen green peas and chopped parsley. Add herbs, pepper and salt if needed. Mix everything together and pour into pie pan lined with dough. Roll out remaining half of dough about 1 inch wider than pie pan, cut a ½ inch hole in the middle and place over the top of the pie, and crimp the edges as you like. For fewer calories, omit the bottom crust. Bake pie at 375 degrees on the middle rack for 1 hour or until it is bubbling in the middle. Remove from oven, let it cool for 5-10 minutes, serve and enjoy. This will keep in the refrigerator and make great leftovers for a few days. Do not freeze after baked. If you want to make it ahead, you can freeze it before you bake it and just bake it while frozen, but add more cooking time. Enjoy!

*Note, alcohol will never cook out completely, so avoid it if you do not wish to consume any alcohol.

Oven "Fried" Chicken

This is a low fat and less messy version of fried chicken! The crust is thinner, but still crispy and delicious! Brining the chicken for 2-48 hours prior to cooking makes it very moist and flavorful so, start 1-2 days ahead.

Yields: 1 chicken cut up

1 Chicken, organic and free range, cut up with bones

Brine (see index)

juice of 1 lemon

4 cups oat or barley or rice or soy flour

4 Tablespoons poultry seasoning or Herbs d' Provence or Italian dried seasoning or a dry rub

kosher or sea salt/black pepper, freshly ground

extra virgin olive oil or grapeseed oil, approximately 1/3 cup

If you buy kosher chicken you can skip the brine. Otherwise, prepare the brine and soak the chicken 2-48 hours in the refrigerator. This will make the chicken much more flavorful, tender and moist.

Preheat oven to 375 degrees. Remove chicken from brine and place on a baking sheet. Discard brine down the kitchen sink and wash everything very well with hot water and soap to kill the bacteria from the raw chicken. Wash lemon, cut in half and squeeze juice over chicken evenly. Let the lemon juice marinate the chicken for 5 minutes. Put the flour into a large plastic zip bag. Sprinkle the chicken evenly with 4 Tablespoons of seasoning, salt and pepper. Place in the flour, seal the bag tightly and shake until well coated. Place chicken onto a baking sheet without them touching each other and drizzle extra virgin olive oil or grapeseed oil over them until they are lightly coated and all the flour is covered, but not so much that it is sitting in a puddle of oil. Bake immediately for 30-45 minutes or until internal temperature is 165 degrees when thermometer is inserted into the middle of the piece of chicken. Note: the smaller pieces will cook faster so, start to check them at 30 minutes and remove pieces when they are done. You may need to leave the thighs and breasts in longer than the drumsticks and wings. Serve with mashed potatoes (see index) or baked potatoes and a salad or green vegetable! If you are in a Southern mood, serve with sautéed kale (see index), candied sweet potatoes (see index) and cornbread (see index). Mmm, mmm, finger licking good!

Rack of Lamb

Spring Lamb is mild and a nice alternative to beef-the other red meat! Garlic, rosemary, Dijon mustard and ground nuts create a flavorful, crispy topping for a rack of lamb.

Yields: 1 rack of lamb, serves 2

1 rack of lamb, best in the springtime

¼ cup Dijon mustard, no preservatives

3 Tablespoons fresh rosemary, chopped

2-3 cloves garlic, crushed

½ cup "parmesan" (see index) or ground nuts (raw almonds, pistachios, hazelnuts)

2 Tablespoons extra virgin olive oil

sea salt and freshly ground black pepper

If lamb is frozen, defrost in refrigerator for 12-24 hours. Rinse lamb in cold water and pat dry with paper towels. Salt and pepper the lamb on both sides. Preheat oven to 375 degrees. In a bowl, whisk mustard, rosemary and garlic together and spread evenly over fat side of the lamb. In another bowl, mix "parmesan" and olive oil together and pour over the mustard and pack it down evenly. Place on a baking sheet or dish and bake on the middle rack of the oven for approximately 10 minutes or until the internal temperature is 140 degrees (medium rare) in the center of the chops. Remove from oven and cover tightly with foil and rest for 10 minutes. Cut in between the bones and serve. Great served with mashed potatoes (see index) and sautéed greens or Brussel sprouts (see index).

Roasted Turkey

I promise this will be the best turkey you will ever make and you will know that baking at a high temperature is the secret to crispy skin and very moist inside! Serve with gravy (see index).

Thawing times:

Always thaw in the refrigerator to prevent bacterial growth.

Defrost in brine. Allow 24 hours per 5 lbs., 20 lbs will take 4 days, 10 lbs will take 2 days.

Roasting Times: It is very important to use an oven thermometer and a digital read thermometer

450 degrees

10-13 lbs 2 ¾ - 3 hours

14-17 lbs 3 - 3 ¼ hours

18-21 lbs 3 ¼ - 3 ½ hours

22-24 lbs 3 ½ - 3 ¾ hours

Times will vary.

Check the turkey in half the time you think it will take; sometimes they surprise you. You can always cook it longer, but you can go back! If you have a convection oven, you're lucky, use the air circulation, and it will take about half the time of the above estimates.

Thermometer for turkey

Oven thermometer

Brine (see index)

1 Turkey-kosher or organic free range, do not use anything else. If Kosher, skip the brining process since it has already been done.

Fresh herbs and citrus or stuffing (see index)

Extra Virgin Olive Oil

Remove innards and wash turkey with cold water, keep the neck and gizzards in a plastic zip bag in the refrigerator to make gravy. Discard the liver. Make brine in a large plastic bucket with a lid. Soak the turkey in brine for two days-keep refrigerated between 36-40 degrees. Drain and dry with paper towels.

Preheat oven to 450 degrees. Loosely fill the cavity with fresh herbs and whole citrus or stuffing. Place a rack in a roasting pan. Rub oil all over turkey, tie legs together with butcher string. Cover with cheesecloth soaked in oil which will keep it moist and allow it to brown. Roast until internal temperature is 165 degrees when thermometer is inserted in the middle of the thigh away from the bone, it will keep cooking to about 175-180 after resting. Take it out at 165 degrees. Cover with aluminum foil and cool on a rack or board. Remove stuffing to a bowl, and put into 150-degree oven to keep warm. Rest turkey for

20-30 minutes so the juices will stay in the meat and not run out. This will make a really juicy turkey, and worth the wait.

Finally, and most importantly, wash all boards, counters etc... with hot water and soap.

Be sure to wash your hands after handling raw poultry to avoid cross contamination

Refrigerate the leftovers as soon as possible to minimize bacterial growth and food borne illness.

Scalloped Ham and Potatoes

A childhood favorite of my sister and me! Hope you enjoy these creamy potatoes and ham as either a main dish or a side dish. Make ahead and reheat just before serving in the microwave or oven.

Yields: 4-6 servings or one 2 quart soufflé dish or 8x8 baking dish

6-8 large Russet or Yukon gold potatoes

1 double recipe of "cream" sauce (see index) use almond milk or chicken broth

1 cooked ham steak* (no nitrates), ¼ inch cubes

Make the "cream" sauce and set aside. Preheat oven to 375 degrees. Scrub potatoes with vegetable wash and cold water, rinse well. Slice into ¼ inch slices with a food processor using the slicing blade, a mandolin or by hand with a sharp 8 inch chef's knife. Fan them into a 2 quart round soufflé dish, or an 8x8 glass baking dish so they are overlapping by a ½ inch. Sprinkle ham in between each layer of potatoes as you go along finishing with a layer of just potatoes. Continue to do this in circles or rows until all potatoes are in the dish. Pour cream sauce over potatoes and gently shake so all the sauce will be evenly distributed. Bake on the middle rack of the oven for 1 hour or until bubbling. Place under broiler on the top shelf for 2 minutes or until golden brown. Serve immediately.

*Wellshire Farm is all natural and no nitrates or preservatives, available at Whole Foods Market

Stroganoff

Whether you make this with Buffalo, my favorite, or Beef or Chicken, it is a hearty comforting meal. I first ate Buffalo in Montana and was surprised at how delicious it tasted! It's a great alternative to Beef. Serve over cooked rice noodles (fusilli or penne) or rice with a green vegetable. For you potato lovers, it's good over mashed spuds too!

Yields: 4 servings

"Cream" sauce, double the recipe to equal 3 cups using beef stock (see index)

1 ½ pounds top or bottom round buffalo*, cut into ¼ inch strips across the grain

2 Tablespoons grapeseed oil

1 medium yellow or white onion, small dice

2 cloves garlic, chopped

½ pound crimini mushrooms, washed and sliced ¼ inch thick

½ cup dry sherry

¼ cup organic catsup

Heat a large skillet (with a lid*), stainless steel or cast iron, over medium high heat and add oil. Sauté meat for 2 minutes on each side, remove and set aside. Over medium to medium high heat sauté onion, garlic and mushrooms until soft. Add sherry and boil until it is almost evaporated. Mix catsup into "cream" sauce and pour all of it over mushrooms. Add meat into mushroom mixture and heat everything over medium high heat until it comes to a simmer. Turn down heat to very low to keep at a simmer. Cover and simmer red meat for 1-2 hours or until meat is tender. Chicken will only take 20 minutes. Serve over cooked rice noodles, rice or mashed potatoes (see index).

*If you don't have a lid, you can set a baking sheet on top of the pan. Or you can finish cooking this in a 350 degree oven in a ceramic or glass baking dish with a lid. Chicken or Beef may be used instead of Buffalo.

Buffalo is available at Whole Foods Market or search online (see Resources and websites)

Swedish Meatballs

Whether you are 6 or 96, you will love these tender and flavorful little meatballs covered in gravy. Serve them over mashed potatoes, rice pasta noodles or rice. They make great leftovers and reheat very well.

Yields: 24 meatballs, serves 4

1 lg. organic egg

1/3 cup almond milk

¼ cup grated yellow or white onion

1 clove garlic, grated

½ teaspoon freshly grated whole nutmeg

½ teaspoon ground allspice

¼ teaspoon ground cardamom

1 teaspoon sea salt or kosher salt

Freshly ground pepper to taste

1 pound ground turkey (not all white meat)*

1 Tablespoon olive oil

1 Tablespoon grapeseed oil

2 Tablespoons oat flour

2 cups organic chicken stock or broth*

2 teaspoons fresh dill or 2 Tablespoons fresh parsley, chopped finely

Preheat oven to 350 degrees. Mix first 9 ingredients in an electric mixer with the paddle attachment until combined. Add ground turkey and mix until well combined. With a 2 ounce ice cream scooper, scoop meat mixture onto a 12 inch oven proof or stainless steel or cast iron frying pan. For larger batches, use a baking sheet lined with parchment. Be sure the meatballs have just enough space between them so they don't touch. Bake on middle rack of the oven for 30 minutes. With a pot holder, remove from oven and add oil then flour to center of pan mixing until combined-If you baked the meatballs on a baking sheet, do this in a separate sauté pan. Pour chicken stock/broth into pan and whisk to make gravy. Add meatballs to gravy if they are on a baking sheet. Return to the oven and bake for 30 more minutes. Remove and sprinkle with dill or parsley and serve immediately.

*You can substitute ground beef or lamb for turkey and use beef stock/broth.

Tempura

This was my favorite dish to order at a Japanese restaurant as a child, and I was so sad, as an adult, when I couldn't find it anywhere that it was wheat free. So, here it is to enjoy at home! This is a really fun stay at home "dinner date"-be creative with the table setting etc...

Yields: 4 servings

4 quarts peanut or vegetable oil

1 recipe of Tempura batter (see index)

16 ounces (1 pound) peeled raw shrimp, tail on and thawed

1 cup fresh green beans or snap peas in shell, washed and dried

1 large yam or sweet potato, washed and ¼ inch slices (peeling is optional)

1 cup Japanese eggplant, sliced ¼ inch thick

1 cup broccoli florets, washed and dried

Be sure to wash all vegetables well and dry them completely or the batter will not stick. They will cook faster if they are room temperature. Rinse and dry the shrimp completely. I am not a fan of disposable things, but I really love paper towels for this recipe! Place 3 layers of paper towels on a baking sheet and set it next to the stove. Pour 4 quarts of oil into

63

a large stock pot, put thermometer on the side of the pot with the end just above the bottom or the pot. Heat the oil on high heat to 300 degrees. Turn down heat to medium for oil to reach 350 degrees for frying. Make batter. Dip shrimp into batter for a light coating, let excess drip off. Very carefully and slowly lower shrimp into the top of the 350 degree oil and let go-moving your hands away very quickly. This will splatter. Cook shrimp for 2 minutes, no longer or they will be rubbery. Using a wire mesh ladle with a long handle to remove the food, allow excess oil to drip into pot and then place them on the paper towel lined baking sheet to drain. Be sure to adjust the heat to keep the oil at 350 degrees which will create a seal around the batter to that it will not absorb too much oil and be greasy. Keep the baking sheet in the oven on the lowest setting to keep everything warm while cooking the remaining batches of vegetables. Continue to cook each vegetable, first the green beans, second yams, third eggplant and finally broccoli. They will all take 1-3 minutes-you want them to still be slightly firm and not mushy. Set a timer for 1 minute and then remove one and test it with a fork. Careful, don't burn your tongue! Be sure to scoop out any stray batter after every vegetable is cooked so you don't have bits of burned batter.

For dipping sauce: use a combination of Tamari (wheat-free soy sauce), Mirin, and Ponzu. Mix to your liking. Instead of sauce just squeeze fresh lemon over the tempura. You can also buy sliced ginger to serve on the side. Great served with a good bottle of cold beer or chilled sake.

Tempura Batter

I really missed the occasional fried food, especially tempura. Here is a recipe that is wheat free!

Yields: approximately 4 cups batter

2 lg. organic eggs

2-2 ½ cups rice flour (white works best)

1 ½ cups sparkling water or good bottled beer

Be sure to have all your vegetables and shrimp etc... washed, cut and ready to go into the batter. Also be sure your oil is at 300 degrees before you begin making this batter. While making the batter let the oil come to 350 degrees before frying to prevent greasy food. See Tempura recipe.

In a large bowl, whisk eggs until beaten. Whisk in 2 cups flour and then slowly pour in sparkling water or beer and stir until smooth, no lumps. If the batter is too thin, add more rice flour. Enjoy!

Vegetables

Brussel Sprouts

I must admit, I hated these little buggars as a child, and an adult, until I changed the way I cooked them! I had them sautéed and seasoned like this in a restaurant and politely ate them, and to my pleasant surprise decided I really liked them! Try them and see if you are converted too! They are a nice compliment to Thanksgiving dinner.

Yields: 4 servings

4 cups Brussel sprouts, cut in half lengthwise

2 Tablespoons extra virgin olive oil

1 Tablespoon good capers packed in oil and drained*

1 bunch fresh sage (do not use dried)

sea salt/black pepper

¼ cup water, filtered or bottled

roasted chestnuts*, optional

If you can find Brussel sprouts on the stalk, buy them that way and they will be fresher and tastier. Wash and dry the Brussel sprouts. Cut the bottom ends off and cut in half lengthwise. Pour olive oil into a hot cast iron pan or heavy bottomed sauté pan, and swirl it around to coat the bottom of the pan evenly. Lay Brussel sprouts cut side down in pan and sauté over medium high heat. Slice sage leaves sideways into

1/8 inch strips. Scatter capers and sage evenly over Brussel sprouts. Sprinkle with salt and freshly ground pepper. Add water and cook until Brussel sprouts are soft with a little resistance, but not hard, when a knife is inserted. Do not cover them. Taste and add salt and pepper to your liking. Serve immediately and enjoy.

*In the fall and winter add chopped roasted chestnuts at the end

*The best capers in oil are at www.jonesandbones. com

Candied Sweet Potatoes

Sweet and creamy with a hint of cinnamon and orange-yum! Perfect for Thanksgiving and fantastic with Fried Chicken (see index)! These take me back to New Orleans!

Yields: 4, ½ cup servings or 2 cups

2 medium sized sweet potatoes or yams, cut into 2-inch chunks

1 cup water

½ cup real maple syrup

2 Tablespoons orange blossom honey

2 Tablespoons blood orange olive oil*

1 ½ teaspoons real vanilla extract

juice and zest of ½ lemon

One cinnamon stick

In a 1-quart saucepan combine all ingredients except olive oil. Cover and cook over medium heat for 30 minutes, stirring occasionally. Uncover and cook 10 minutes, stir constantly or it will stick. Remove cinnamon stick. Add blood orange olive oil and stir. Serve immediately.

* Available at www.jonesandbones.com, or use grapeseed or olive oil and zest of one washed orange, and use ¾ cup water and ¼ cup fresh squeezed orange juice

Carrots and Parsnips

This is a match made in Heaven, and really good restaurants! As children we all heard, eat your carrots and vegetables...they are good for you! Well, they are good for us, high in antioxidants, and they are delicious when they are not overcooked to mush and seasoned well. Give these a try, and you'll change your mind, and your kids, about vegetables!

Yields: varies, 1 carrot and 1 parsnip per person

organic carrots

organic parsnips

extra virgin olive oil or grapeseed oil

kosher or sea salt

Pepper grinder

ground cumin in shaker bottle with a shaker top, optional

flat leaf parsley, finely chopped, optional

Preheat oven to 400 degrees, if you are really hurried 450 degrees will speed up the cooking. Scrub carrots and parsnips with vegetable wash and rinse well. Leave the peel on the carrots since that is where the most vitamins and minerals are found. Peel the parsnips because the peel can be bitter. Cut off tops and discard. Using a sharp knife and cutting board, cut carrots and parsnips into ½ inch slices, diagonally. Place on a metal baking pan or glass baking dish, but metal will brown better. Drizzle just enough extra virgin olive oil or grapeseed oil to lightly coat them-please no puddles of oil. Sprinkle kosher salt or sea salt and grind black pepper. If you are using cumin, shake it over the carrots and parsnips for a light dusting-this is a very strong spice and should be used in moderation. Bake on the second from the top rack of the oven for approximately 10 minutes. Check by inserting a fork into the carrots and parsnips-if they are soft but still a little resistant or crunchy...they are done. Don't wait for them to be completely soft unless you are going to puree them. Sprinkle fresh chopped parsley over the carrots and parsnips just before serving. Parsley is pretty but also very healthy. I purposely did not include amounts in the recipe because I want to teach you to cook things for various portions. Baking is a different story, and exact measurement is crucial!

"Creamed" Vegetables

A quick and easy vegetarian meal that is very comforting. The mushrooms have a similar texture to meat and make this a hearty main dish.

Yields: 2-4 servings

1 recipe of "cream" sauce (see index)-using vegetable stock

1 Tablespoon extra virgin olive oil or grapeseed oil

1 stalk celery, small dice

1 carrot, ¼ inch slices

3 cups assorted mushrooms (crimini, portabella, morel, chanterelle, king etc...), quartered

1 Tablespoon dry sherry, optional

½ cup frozen green peas

fresh parsley, chopped, optional

1 cup cooked rice (jasmine, basmati or brown) or 2 cups cooked rice penne pasta or quinoa

Cook rice, pasta or quinoa, set aside. Make "cream" sauce and set aside. Wash and dry mushrooms-I like to use a mushroom brush and then a damp paper towel. Sauté celery and carrots in oil over high heat for 2 minutes. Add mushrooms and sauté over medium high heat until soft. Stir in 1 Tablespoon sherry, cook until almost evaporated-about 30 seconds or less.

Pour "cream" sauce over vegetables. Stir in green peas. Heat over medium heat just until hot. Serve over cooked rice, quinoa or cooked rice penne pasta. Garnish with fresh chopped parsley.

French Fries

I was amazed when I tasted these French Fries in culinary school because the texture and taste was the best I'd ever had, and I learned why!

Yields: 4 servings or more

4 Idaho potatoes, peeled and cut into ½ strips

2 cups oil (grapeseed or peanut or duck fat)

Sea salt

Dipping sauces: ketchup (Shh-don't tell the French), aioli (garlic mayonnaise)

Prepare the dipping sauces and set aside. Be creative add basil pesto or curry powder to mayonnaise. Add hot sauce to ketchup or Jamaican jerk seasoning to ketchup. Have fun!

Peel potatoes and cut ends off and cut lengthwise into ½ in strips. Pull them apart in the center and place them flat side down so you have two piles of potatoes. Cut them again lengthwise into ½ inch strips that resemble French fries. The goal is to cut them in uniform strips so they will cook evenly. Heat the oil or fat to 285 degrees in a 10 inch cast iron pan. In France they often use duck fat to fry the French fries and that is why they taste so good! Gently place the potatoes in the oil and fry for 10 minutes. Keep your eye on the thermometer and adjust the temperature to hold the oil at 285 degrees. Remove the fries from the oil and drain on a paper towel lined baking sheet. Increase the heat of the oil to 350 degrees. Gently put the potatoes back into the oil and fry until golden brown. Remove from oil and drain on new paper towels. Sprinkle with sea salt or kosher salt and freshly ground pepper. Serve immediately. There is nothing worse than cold French fries, in my humble opinion. Bon Appetite!

Mashed Potatoes

Everyone loves Mashed Potatoes! Here is one without the cream and butter, but just as flavorful, creamy and fluffy! Even better with gravy.

Yields: 4 servings

1 Gallon of cold water

1 Tablespoon sea salt

4 Russet or large Yukon Gold potatoes (1large per person)

Chicken or vegetable stock (1/4 cup to 4 potatoes)

Olive oil or vegan Earth Balance (2 Tablespoons per 4 potatoes)

Optional add INs: grated or shaved black truffles, pesto, roasted garlic*

Peel and wash potatoes. Cut potatoes into 2 inch cubes**, and put into large pot of cold water and 1 Tablespoon sea salt. Bring to a boil; cook until potatoes are soft when pierced with a toothpick or fork-about 10 minutes. While potatoes are cooking, heat chicken stock or vegetable stock. Drain potatoes. Put potatoes into an electric stand mixer with paddle attachment or put through a food mill for the best texture. Beat until smooth and fluffy. While machine is running, slowly pour stock into potatoes. Then, pour some olive oil or vegan Earth

Balance into potatoes. Season with salt and pepper if needed. Stir in any additions you like. Serve with gravy (see index)!

*If you want to use raw garlic add with potatoes to cold water and boil

**If you are in a hurry, cut the potatoes into smaller chunks and they will cook faster

Roasted Beets

Roasting beets concentrates their flavor and sweetness and retains the nutrients. These are nothing like canned beets. You will love how sweet and flavorful they will be!

Yields: 4 (1/2 cup) servings

4 large beets or 2 cups baby beets

2 Tablespoons grapeseed oil

sea salt/pepper, to taste

juice and zest of 1 orange

1 Tablespoon good balsamic vinegar*

2 Tablespoons extra virgin olive oil, plain or orange*

Preheat oven to 400 degrees. Scrub beets with vegetable wash, rinse well and dry. Cut off tops, if attached, and reserve them to sauté. Do not peel them. Rub beets with enough grapeseed oil to coat them. Place on a baking sheet and put on the second from the top shelf of the oven. Depending on their size the roasting time will vary. Check them after 20 minutes of baking and then every 10 minutes thereafter. They are done when a skewer or paring knife is inserted in the middle and they are soft all the way through. Remove from oven and cool until you can touch them without getting burned. Put on a pair of plastic or rubber gloves or you will have red hands for a few days. Peel the beets by pushing on the skin and it should slip right off! Aren't you glad you didn't peel them? Cut the stem off and discard. Slice the beets in round slices ¼ inch thick or in ½ inch wedges. If using baby beets, cut them in half.

While the beets are roasting or cooling, place orange juice, zest, balsamic vinegar, salt and pepper into a bowl and whisk to combine. While whisking the liquid slowly add the olive oil to make a dressing. Pour this onto the warm beets after they are cut. Serve hot or cold. Great for a picnic!

*Very good balsamic vinegar and olive oils available at www.jonesandbones.com or Whole Foods Market.

Roasted Rutabaga and Turnips

Roasting vegetables is so easy and they are crispy on the outside and tender on the inside.

Yields: 4 (1/2 cup) servings

1 large rutabaga and/or 2 large turnips*

sea salt/pepper, to taste

2 sprigs fresh thyme

2 Tablespoons extra virgin olive oil or grapeseed oil

2 sprigs of thyme, for garnish

Preheat oven to 400 degrees. Cut stem off rutabaga and peel with a vegetable peeler. With a very sharp 10-12 inch chef's knife, cut rutabaga in half from top to bottom. Put cut side down, so it doesn't wobble around, and cut in ½ inch wedges and then dice into ½ inch chunks by cutting wedges sideways. Repeat the same steps for turnips. *Turnips and rutabaga cook at different rates, so put them on separate baking sheets. Drizzle with olive oil and toss to coat evenly. Sprinkle with salt and freshly ground pepper to taste. Put fresh sprigs of thyme wedged in between the chunks of rutabaga. Place on a baking sheet and put on the second from the top shelf of the oven. Check them after 20 minutes of baking and then every 10 minutes thereafter-could take up to 45 minutes. They are done when a skewer or knife is inserted in the middle and they are soft all the way through. Taste and adjust seasoning. Remove the leaves of thyme by holding the sprig by the top and pulling downward with your thumb and fingers. Sprinkle thyme leaves over rutabaga and/or turnips. Serve immediately.

If you have never had these vegetables before give them a try. Rutabagas are sweet and turnips are a little spicy or hot like a radish. Their texture is similar to potatoes. Expand your culinary repertoire and add these vegetables to your menu. They can also be boiled in salted water and served in chunks or pureed with olive oil drizzled over them. You can also add them to soup, but remember turnips take longer to cook than rutabagas so, add the turnips first and when they are about halfway cooked add the rutabagas.

Sautéed Corn

Stopping at the farm stand to buy fresh corn was such a treat as a child. You cannot compare fresh corn to canned or frozen. Fresh corn on the cob is so sweet and crunchy. I like to cut it off the cob so it is easier to eat and doesn't get stuck in between my teeth! Sautéing is faster and tastier than boiling-you'll see!

Yields: 4 servings

1 Tablespoon plain or lime extra virgin olive oil or grapeseed oil*

4 cobs fresh corn

4 sprigs fresh thyme or ½ teaspoon dried thyme

sea salt/black pepper, freshly ground, to taste

zest 1 lime

juice ½ fresh lime

1 shallot, finely diced

Wash lime, zest with microplane grater and set aside. Juice ½ of it, set aside. Shuck husks and silk off the corn cobs. Wash the corn and dry. Stand the corn up on end, on a wooden cutting board with a silicone pot holder under the board so it does not slip, and carefully cut along the cob, from top to bottom, to remove the kernels-a sharp 8 inch knife works best. Discard cobs or freeze for corn chowder or vegetable stock. In a sauté pan over high heat, add oil and then corn. Evenly sprinkle with thyme, sea salt and pepper. Cook for 2 minutes. Squeeze lime juice, stir in zest and serve immediately. You may never boil corn again after tasting this delicious sautéed corn.

*See Resources for olive oils

Sautéed Kale

Kale is a wonderful vegetable that is packed with vitamins and calcium.

Yields: 2-4 servings

1 bunch kale (any variety) dino is my favorite

2 Tablespoons extra virgin olive oil

1 clove fresh garlic, sliced thinly

sea salt or ume plum vinegar*

freshly ground black pepper

Cut the kale leaves in 1 inch horizontal strips, discard tough stems. Wash well in cold water and spin in a salad spinner. Heat the oil over medium heat in large sauté pan. Add garlic and cook over medium heat for 1 minute. Add kale, sea salt or ume plum vinegar and pepper. Sauté 1 minute then stir and turn over. When all kale is wilted and soft it is cooked. Serve immediately.

*Ume plum vinegar is made by brining Japanese plums in salt. It is very flavorful and a great substitute for salt when sautéing vegetables.

Sautéed Spinach

Sautéing is so much faster and tastier than boiling. Try this and you won't go back to boiling! As children we all heard that spinach is good for us and it is...it's loaded with iron!

Yields: 2 servings

1 Tablespoon olive oil

1 shallot, optional

1 clove garlic, optional

1 bag washed spinach, baby is best

pinch sea salt or 6 drops ume plum vinegar*

freshly ground black pepper

Wash the spinach and spin in a salad spinner. Be sure the spinach is completely dry before sautéing or the oil will splatter. In a large sauté pan heat the oil over medium high heat add shallot and sauté 1 minute. Add garlic and spinach, sauté 1 minute add salt or 6 drops of ume vinegar and pepper and turn over. Sauté for 1 more minute or until it is wilted. Serve immediately.

*Ume vinegar is made by brining Japanese plums in salt. It is very flavorful and a great substitute for salt when sautéing vegetables.

Sautéed Swiss Chard

Did you know that Chard is packed with vitamins and calcium? I converted all my college friends to eat more greens with this recipe. It is inspired by the Italians who cook it this way.

Yields: 4 servings

1 bunch Swiss chard, rainbow or any color

2 Tablespoons extra virgin olive oil

1 clove fresh garlic, sliced thinly

2 Tablespoons pine nuts

2 Tablespoons raisins, dark or golden

sea salt or ume plum vinegar*

freshly ground black pepper

Cut the chard leaves in 1 inch horizontal strips, discard tough stems. Wash well in cold water and spin in a salad spinner. Heat the oil over medium heat in large sauté pan. Add garlic, pine nuts and raisins and cook over medium heat for 1 minute. Add chard, sea salt or ume plum vinegar and pepper. Sauté 1 minute then stir and turn over. Be careful the pine nuts burn quickly. When all chard is wilted and soft it is cooked. Serve immediately.

*Ume plum vinegar is made by brining Japanese

plums in salt. It is very flavorful and a great substitute for salt when sautéing vegetables.

Scalloped Potatoes

Another dish I have really missed until now! Hope you enjoy these creamy potatoes as side dish. Make ahead and reheat just before serving in the microwave or oven.

Yields: 4-6 servings, one soufflé dish

4-6 large russet or Yukon gold potatoes

2 Tablespoons fresh herbs (thyme, rosemary, oregano), chopped

1 double recipe of "cream" sauce (see index) use almond milk or chicken broth

Make the "cream" sauce and set aside. Preheat oven to 375 degrees. Scrub potatoes with vegetable wash and cold water, rinse well. Slice into ¼ inch slices with a food processor using the slicing blade, a mandolin or by hand with a sharp 8 inch chef's knife. Fan them into a 2 quart round soufflé dish, or an 8x8 glass baking dish so they are overlapping by ¼ to ½ inch. Sprinkle fresh chopped herbs over each layer of potatoes ending with a layer of just potatoes. Continue to do this in circles or rows until all potatoes are in the dish. Pour cream sauce over potatoes and gently shake so all the sauce will be distributed evenly. Bake on the middle rack of the oven for 1 hour or until bubbling and potatoes are tender when pierced with a skewer or knife. Place under broiler on the top shelf for 2 minutes or until golden brown. Serve immediately.

Sauces/Sides/Soups/ Salad Dressings

Applesauce

You will never want to buy applesauce after you taste this and realize how fast and easy it is to make yourself!

Yield: 4 cups

4 lbs. apples, McIntosh or Granny Smith or Golden Delicious or combination

1/2 cup agave nectar or honey

2 whole cinnamon sticks

1 Tablespoon fresh lemon juice

Peel, core and quarter the apples. Place in a saucepan with just enough cold water to cover the bottom of the pan. Add the cinnamon sticks. Bring to a simmer, cover and cook until the apples are tender, approximately 15 minutes. Stir in the agave or honey and lemon juice. Simmer uncovered for 10 minutes. Remove cinnamon sticks and press the apples through a food mill or process in a food processor for a smooth applesauce. You can leave the sauce chunky if you like. Serve warm or cold. For a low fat dessert, add a 2 ounce scoop of vanilla ice "cream" (see index) to ½ cup applesauce-tastes like apple pie!

Basil Pesto

This is not only for pasta, but is a great marinade for chicken and shrimp too! Yes, you can have pasta again!

Yields: approximately 1 ½-2 cups

1 large bunch or 2 small bunches fresh basil

¼ cup pine nuts

2 cloves garlic, peeled

1 cup good extra virgin olive oil*

sea salt/pepper, to taste

"parmesan" topping (see index)

Wash basil well. Pick off the leaves and dry them. Put basil leaves into a food processor, and chop with the s blade. Add pine nuts, garlic a pinch of salt and 10 grinds of pepper. Blend all of this up until finely chopped. While processor is running, slowly pour olive oil into feed tube. When it is all blended, and the consistency you want, it is finished. Taste and adjust seasoning.

*spend the money and get a really good tasting bottle of olive oil, not the stuff on the bottom shelf of the grocery store that is under $10 for a huge bottle! This is your flavoring so it is worth it to invest in a good tasting extra virgin olive oil since your dish will taste like it.

Serve over cooked rice pasta or quinoa pasta and sprinkle "parmesan" (see index) topping over it. Stir into cooked quinoa. Marinate chicken or shrimp and grill on the barbeque. Add to mayonnaise for a tasty sandwich spread. Be creative!

This can be made in a blender, but the food processor works best. If you do use a blender, finely chop the basil first.

Cranberry Sauce

This sauce is so quick and easy to make and much better than the stuff in the can!

Yields: approximately 2 cups

1 bag whole fresh cranberries*

1 cup fresh squeezed orange juice or water

zest of 1 washed organic orange

½ cup agave nectar

1 Tablespoon orange marmalade, optional

1 teaspoon real vanilla extract

Wash cranberries in a colander and pick out any bruised or soft ones and discard. Put all of the ingredients into a 2 quart saucepot and bring to a boil, stir. When most of the cranberries have popped, it is done. I like a chunky sauce so I do not let them all burst. This will take about 10 minutes. Cool to room temperature and pour into glass jars. Refrigerate. Serve cold or warm. It is not only for Thanksgiving, but great on chicken all year round.

*purchase an extra bag and freeze for later in the year when they are out of season

"Cream" Sauce

This sauce is one of the 5 Mother sauces that is the basis to create all other sauces in French cooking. It is my version of Béchamel, but is really a Volute. It can be used for any recipe using a white cream sauce.

Yields: 1-2 cups

¼ cup finely chopped yellow or white onion or shallot*

2 Tablespoons grapeseed oil or vegan Earth Balance

2 Tablespoons oat flour

1-2 cups almond milk or chicken stock or vegetable stock (depending on the recipe)**

1 bay leaf

1 teaspoon dried thyme or 1 Tablespoon fresh thyme

1/16 teaspoon freshly grated nutmeg

sea salt/pepper to taste

In a 2 quart saucepot over medium-high heat, add oil. Sauté onion in oil until it is translucent. Whisk in flour and cook for 2 minutes, whisking constantly. Quickly pour almond milk or stock, while whisking, the pot-be careful, it will splatter. Bring to a boil and whisk until it is very smooth and thick. Add bay leaf, nutmeg, and salt/pepper. Turn down to low heat and simmer, cook for 5 minutes. Strain through a fine mesh sieve for a more velvety texture. This will thicken quickly.

**Add more almond milk or stock if it is too thick until desired consistency.

Use stock when making a savory dish such as creamed tuna or chicken

*For more flavor: Cut an onion in half and simmer it covered in the almond milk or stock with bay leaf for 10 minutes.

Hollandaise Sauce

Ah, yes you can have Eggs Benedict again!

Yields: approximately ¾ cup-serves 4

2 lg. organic egg yolks

1 Tablespoon fresh squeezed lemon juice (do not use bottled)

6 Tablespoons vegan Earth Balance, frozen cut into Tablespoons

1/16-1/8 teaspoon Tabasco or hot sauce or cayenne pepper, to your taste

Fill a saucepan half way up and bring water to a simmer. Place a heatproof glass bowl (not metal) over the simmering water and whisk in yolks and lemon juice. Continue whisking and add one Tablespoon of vegan Earth Balance at a time until it is all combined. Remove from heat and add Tabasco or hot sauce or cayenne pepper. Serve immediately.

Note: this will be salty, so do not add any additional salt.

Honey Spread

This is delicious on cornbread, Irish Soda Bread, scones and biscuits.

Yields: ¾ cup+

1 stick vegan Earth Balance

¼ cup honey or agave nectar

In an electric mixer, fitted with a paddle, mix ingredients together until light and fluffy. Be sure to stop the mixer a few times and scrape down the sides and bottom of the bowl. Keep in refrigerator in a glass dish with a lid.

Raspberry Sauce

This is a delicious dessert sauce that will look beautiful too! For a match made in Heaven, serve with chocolate cake or over ice "cream", or in ice "cream" soda! Great over fresh fruit too.

Yields: 2 cups

16 ounces or 2 cups fresh or frozen raspberries, organic when possible

¼ cup agave nectar

1 teaspoon fresh lemon juice

1 teaspoon real vanilla extract

Place raspberries, lemon juice and agave in a 2 quart saucepot and bring to a boil over high heat. Stir until raspberries have fallen apart. Remove from heat and stir in vanilla. Stain through a fine sieve while still hot. Cool to room temperature off the heat and serve. Store the sauce in a plastic squeeze bottle and refrigerate for up to 1 week. You can make dots, lines and designs on a dinner plate to serve with your chocolate cake or dessert. This is also great with the lemon meringue tart (see index). Enjoy!

Reduction Sauce

Serve this sauce with any meat and or mashed potatoes. It will add lots of flavor and transform any plain dish into a gourmet meal! Make this while your meat is cooking or ahead of time.

Yields: 1 ½ cups

1 Tablespoon fat cut off meat (duck, chicken, lamb)

1 teaspoon extra virgin olive oil

½ onion, diced finely

1 clove garlic, sliced

¼ cup ruby port

1 cup good red wine

2 cups stock (chicken, duck, vegetable)

1 sprig fresh rosemary

2 sprigs fresh thyme or ½ teaspoon dried

½ cup dried cherries or cranberries, optional

freshly ground black pepper to taste

1 teaspoon arrowroot or cornstarch or tapioca starch dissolved in 1 Tablespoon cold water

In a 2 quart saucepot, pour oil and render fat on low heat until all the fat has come out. Discard piece of fat. Sauté onion in fat over medium to high heat until it is translucent. Add garlic to onions and sauté until golden brown-be careful it will burn quickly. Add port and red wine and cook for one minute. Add stock, herbs, pepper and dried cherries. Stir and bring to a boil, then turn down to a simmer over low heat. Cook uncovered over low heat until it is reduced by half. Bring back to a boil and pour in starch/water mixture, whisk until smooth. Cook for 2 minutes. Season sauce with salt and pepper to taste. Remove sprigs of rosemary and thyme. Serve hot. You can pour a tablespoon of the sauce onto the plate and lay slices of meat fanned out over it. Spoon a little of the sauce on top of the meat and mashed potatoes. If you have any left over, refrigerate.

Turkey Brine

Brining makes a turkey so moist and flavorful, it is worth the time.

2 gallons cold water, do not use hot water

2 cups kosher or sea salt

1-cup sucanat or ¾ cup agave nectar, optional

Mix all ingredients together in a large container*. Submerge the turkey, innards removed, into the brine, and be sure it is completely covered with water. Place a dinner place on top to hold it under water. Cover and refrigerate, on the bottom shelf, for 18-48 hours. I submerge the frozen turkey into the brine and let it defrost this way. The brine will make the turkey very juicy. Drain and pat dry just before roasting. Proceed as you normally would. See Roasted Turkey recipe. This can also be done with chicken.

* Restaurant supplies have great plastic round bucket containers with lids, which is ideal for this project.

Turkey Gravy

This is so much better than anything you could ever buy; and is well worth the time! After your guests/family tastes this, they will be asking for you to make the gravy every year! Mom, thank you for teaching me how to make this delicious gravy!

Yields: approximately 2-4 cups depending on how much stock is used

1-2 turkey necks*

4-8 cups chicken stock (not broth)

2 teaspoons tapioca starch** mixed in 1 Tablespoon of cold water or 1 Tablespoon of oat flour mixed with ¼ cup cold water

Put turkey necks and stock in a 4 quart saucepot. Bring to a boil over high heat and turn down to low heat and simmer uncovered until the meat falls off the bone, approximately 20 minutes.

Save the liquid. Take out the necks and cool on a plate. With a fork scrape off all the meat, discard bones. Put all the meat and liquid into a blender-only fill the blender ¾ of the way full and seal the lid very tightly. While holding the top on tightly, blend on low and then medium to high until smooth. There will be some small pieces of meat, and that's ok. Set this aside.

After the turkey comes out of the oven, put the turkey on a platter, cover with aluminum foil to rest for 20 minutes so the juice will be reabsorbed into the meat and not run out when you slice it. Drain off the grease from the pan drippings; gravy separators are great. Put 2 Tablespoons oat flour and ¼ cup cold water or 2 teaspoons tapioca starch with 1 Tablespoon of cold water into a jar and shake until there are not lumps and it is mixed well, set aside.

Put the roasting pan onto the stovetop over low heat, pour the stock/neck meat over the pan drippings, and whisk to deglaze the pan. Over high heat bring to a boil and pour flour slurry over the pan juices. Whisk over high heat for approximately 2 minutes or until thick, to get rid of the flour taste. If you like it thicker, make another flour/water mixture, whisk into the gravy and cook for 2 more minutes. Taste and season with salt and pepper. Pour into a gravy boat and enjoy! * I like to make extra gravy for those leftovers! I recommend 2 turkey necks, which you can purchase from the butcher.

**Arrowroot or cornstarch may be substituted

Biscuits

These are very flakey biscuits. No Southern meal is complete without them.

Yields: 9 Biscuits

2 cups oat flour

¼ cup barley flour

2 ½ teaspoons baking powder

½ teaspoon sea salt, fine

½ cup vegan Earth Balance or vegetable shortening, cold

¾ cup coconut milk

Preheat oven to 450 degrees. Sift flour, baking powder and salt into a bowl or food processor. Add Earth Balance or shortening. Using a pastry cutter or food processor blend until the size of course crumbs. Add coconut milk and mix or stir just until combine. On a floured board gently pat/roll out dough to ½ inch think. Cut circles out with a round 2 ½ inch biscuit cutter. Place on a baking sheet and bake on the middle rack of the oven until golden brown, about 12 minutes. Cool for 5 minutes on a wire rack and serve warm. Great with gravy or dipped in stew.

Coconut Rice

This fragrant rice is creamy with a hint of coconut. Perfect with curry!

Yields: serves 4

1 cup filtered or bottled water

1 cup light coconut milk

1 cup basmati or jasmine rice

pinch of sea salt

1 Tablespoon shredded coconut, unsweetened and toasted*

Bring water, salt and coconut milk to a boil over high heat. Add rice and stir. Cover and turn heat down to low and cook for 15 minutes-set a timer. Turn off heat and let it sit for 5 minutes covered. Uncover, stir in shredded coconut and fluff with a wooden spoon. Serve hot.

*Put coconut under broiler on a baking sheet and broil until golden-watch it closely because it burns quickly!

Cornbread Stuffing

Stuff a Turkey, Chicken, Cornish Game Hens or Goose with this moist and flavorful stuffing.

Yields: enough stuffing for a large Turkey

1 recipe cornbread (see index)

1 medium yellow or white onion, diced

1 cup diced organic celery

1 cup diced organic apples Granny Smith or Pippin or any crunchy variety, cored

½ cup chopped nuts (pecans or walnuts), optional

1 bunch flat leaf parsley, chopped finely

1 Tablespoon poultry seasoning or 2 Tablespoons fresh sage, chopped finely

For a Tex-Mex stuffing, omit apple and add ½ cup diced bell pepper, and chopped cilantro instead of parsley and 1 minced jalapeno (remove seeds)

Cut cornbread into 1 inch cubes and put into a large bowl. In a large skillet, sauté onion and celery until transparent; set aside and cool. Add all ingredients with cornbread and gently mix until combined. Do not put inside the cavity until just before baking since bacteria grows rapidly. Gently put stuffing into cavity, and do not pack it tightly or it will be too dense. Place all the remaining stuffing in an oiled baking dish and bake until hot, approximately 30 minutes. Be sure to remove the stuffing from the cavity after removing it from the oven and keep it in a baking dish in the oven on warm. Refrigerate any unused portions as soon as possible. Reheat leftovers in the microwave or covered in the oven. If it is dry you can add a little chicken stock. Eat your stuffing and enjoy! You can be creative and add anything you like to this stuffing-mushrooms, oysters etc...

Hummus

Serve this protein packed spread with fresh cut raw vegetables and apples. Spread onto a wheat-free tortilla and add shredded veggies and baby lettuce to create a roll up.

Yields: approximately 2-2 ½ cups

2 (16oz cans) garbanzo beans*, drained and rinsed

Juice and zest of 1 organic lemon

2 garlic cloves, chopped

2 Tablespoons tahini (sesame paste)

sea salt

water, preferably filtered or bottled

¼ cup extra virgin olive oil or lemon olive oil

½ teaspoon sumac (Middle Eastern spice), optional

paprika for garnish

In a food processor with the chopping blade, combine garbanzo beans, lemon juice, garlic, tahini, sumac and salt mix until smooth. Slowly pour the olive oil through the feed tube, while the processor is running. It will be thick so, add a little water through the feed tube until you get the right consistency. Blend until very smooth. Pour into a serving bowl and drizzle with olive oil and sprinkle with a little paprika. Enjoy!

You should adjust the amount of all the ingredients to your taste. You can add more or less of the garlic, lemon juice or tahini. I like a little garlic and a lot of lemon!

*Instead of Garbanzo beans, use cooked/canned white beans, black beans, kidney beans or edamame.

For additional flavors:

Add ¼ cup sundried tomatoes packed in oil and drained or reconstituted or

2 Tablespoons basil pesto (see index)

"Parmesan" Topping

A very healthy alternative to Parmesan cheese with a similar flavor and texture! This is great over salad or rice pasta. Use this topping in place of bread crumbs on fish or meat too. Brazil nuts are very high in selenium and zinc!

Yields: 2 cups

1 cup Brazil nuts, whole

1 cup hazelnuts, whole

1 clove fresh garlic, whole, optional

½ teaspoon sea salt

Place all ingredients into a food processor and blend until the consistency of bread crumbs. Refrigerate in a glass jar or plastic zip bag. Sprinkle on pasta or over salad. Use as a coating for thin slices of fish, poultry or meat in place of bread crumbs and sauté over medium-high heat.

Potato Gnocchi

These gnocchi are light and fluffy little pillows of goodness. Top with basil pesto, marinara sauce or olive oil and garlic. Serve as a side dish or a main course.

Yields: 6 main course servings or 12 appetizer or side dish servings

2 pounds red potatoes

2 cups oat flour

2 teaspoons sea salt

Fill a large pot with cold water ¾ of the way to the top. Wash potatoes with vegetable wash and rinse well. Cut potatoes into small pieces and put into the pot of water. Over high heat, bring potatoes to a boil, keep uncovered, add salt and stir. Boil until tender when fork is inserted, about 10 minutes. Drain potatoes through strainer or colander. Put the potatoes through a food mill or potato ricer. Put potatoes into an electric stand mixer and add oat flour. Mix with the paddle attachment until well combined. Wash large pot or get out another clean large pot and fill with water and bring to a boil over high heat. Take a handful of the potato mixture at a time and form into a log. Roll until ½ inch thick. If it falls apart, squeeze it together between the palm of your hand and fingers-like when you played with playdough! Roll until smooth. Cut into ½ inch pieces. Slowly drop gnocchi into boiling water keeping them from touching each other. They are done when they float to the top, about 1 minute. Remove with a strainer and put into a ceramic or glass dish or bowl. Continue until all of the gnocchi are cooked. Pour hot pesto or sauce over the gnocchi and serve. Once cooked, they can be refrigerated and reheated in the microwave.

Stuffing

Stuff a Turkey, Chicken, Cornish Game Hens or Goose with this moist and flavorful stuffing. Spelt is part of the wheat family and is tolerated by many people who have wheat intolerance.

Yields: enough stuffing for a large Turkey

1 loaf spelt bread, cubed (see index) or 1 loaf of rice bread or 100% rye bread

1 medium yellow or white onion, diced

1 cup diced organic celery

1 cup diced apples Granny Smith or Pippin or any crunchy variety, cored

½ cup dried fruit (raisins, cherries, cranberries, apricots, prunes), optional

½ cup chopped nuts (pecans or walnuts), optional

1 bunch flat leaf parsley, chopped finely

1 Tablespoon poultry seasoning or 2 Tablespoons fresh sage, chopped finely

¼ cup chicken stock

For a Tex-Mex stuffing, omit fruit and add ½ cup diced bell pepper, and chopped cilantro instead of parsley and 1 minced jalapeno (seeded)

Cut bread into 1 inch cubes and put into a large

bowl. In a large skillet, sauté onion and celery until transparent; set aside and cool. Add ingredients with bread and gently mix until combined. Do not put inside the cavity until just before baking since bacteria grows rapidly. Gently put stuffing into cavity, and do not pack it tightly or it will be too dense. Place all the remaining stuffing in an oiled baking dish and bake until hot, approximately 30 minutes. Be sure to remove the stuffing from the cavity after removing it from the oven and keep in a baking dish in the oven on warm. Refrigerate any unused portions as soon as possible. Reheat in the microwave or covered in the oven. If it is dry you can add a little chicken stock. Eat your stuffing and enjoy! You can be creative and add anything you like to this stuffing-mushrooms, oysters etc...

Clam Chowder

The first time I had this was as a small child in New England. This soup is rich and creamy with chunks of potatoes.

Yields: 6-8 servings

2 Tablespoons Grapeseed or Sunflower oil

2 cups yellow or white onion, diced

1 cup fresh fennel, thinly sliced, optional

1 cup celery, diced

3 cups russet or red potatoes, diced

1 teaspoon dried thyme or 3 sprigs fresh thyme

½ teaspoon Old Bay seasoning

½ teaspoon celery seeds

freshly ground black pepper to taste

2 cups clams, cooked

1 bottle clam juice

1 cup water, filtered or bottled

3 Tablespoons oil

½ cup oat flour

1 cup almond, rice or soy milk

2 cups vegetable stock

2 bay leaves

½ bunch fresh flat leaf parsley, chopped

¼ teaspoon fennel seeds or dried tarragon, optional

In a large stock pot, over medium heat saute onions, celery, and fennel in 2 Tablespoons of oil until translucent. Pour clam juice, water and seasonings over onion mixture. Add potatoes and simmer until tender, about 10 minutes. In a small sauce pan add 2 Tablespoons oil. Whisk in flour, cook over medium heat for 2 minutes. Add stock and almond milk while whisking constantly and bring to a boil; then stir into potatoes. Stir in clams. Taste for seasoning, adjust if necessary. Sprinkle the chopped parsley over the top. Serve immediately. Do not cook clams for longer than 1 minute or they will become tough.

Corn Chowder

This soup is the so sweet when corn is at its peak in the summertime.

Yields: 4-6 servings

2 Tbsp. grapeseed or sunflower oil

2 cups yellow or white onion, diced

1 cup fresh fennel, thinly sliced, optional

1 cup celery, diced

3 cups russet or red potatoes, diced

1 tsp. dried thyme or 3 sprigs fresh thyme

½ tsp. Old Bay seasoning

freshly ground black pepper to taste

2 cups fresh corn kernels*

3 Tbsp. grapeseed oil

½ cup oat flour

1 cup almond, rice or soy milk

2 cups vegetable stock

1 cup filtered water

2 bay leaves

½ bunch fresh flat leaf parsley, chopped

¼ tsp. fennel seeds, optional

In a large stock pot, over medium heat saute onions, celery, corn and fennel in 2 Tbsp. of oil until translucent. Pour water and seasonings over onion mixture. Add potatoes and simmer until tender, about 10 minutes. In a small sauce pan add 2 Tbsp. grapeseed oil. Whisk in flour, cook over medium heat for 2 minutes. Add stock and almond milk while whisking constantly and bring to a boil; then stir into potatoes. Taste for seasoning, adjust if necessary. Sprinkle the chopped parsley over the top.

* frozen or canned corn may be used, but fresh is the best

Pureed Vegetable Soup

This is so fast and easy. When I was in culinary school I was a private chef and the couple wanted to have soup every night, so I found an easy way to make small amounts! You don't have to puree the vegetables since it makes a nice broth soup if you prefer.

Yields: serves 2

1 teaspoon grapeseed or extra virgin olive oil, optional

¼ cup diced onion, optional

2 cups fresh or frozen vegetables, diced (peas, squash, corn, broccoli, cauliflower etc...)

3-4 cups chicken or vegetable stock or water

1 teaspoon fresh chopped herbs, optional (thyme, oregano, parsley, sage, tarragon, basil)

sea salt and freshly ground black pepper, to taste

In a 2 quart sauce pot, sauté onion in grapeseed oil until translucent. Add a single vegetable of your choice and stock or water. Bring to a boil over high heat. Simmer over low heat until vegetables are fork tender. Pour into a blender or use a hand stick blender and blend starting on low speed and gradually increasing to high speed. Be sure to hold the lid down with a kitchen towel to be sure the steam doesn't push the lid off! Add fresh herbs. Taste for seasoning and adjust to your own taste. For a silky smooth soup, strain through a fine mesh sieve, but it is not necessary. I like it best strained.

My favorite combinations:

peas and tarragon

squash and sage

corn and thyme

broccoli and basil

carrot and parsley

Caesar Salad Dressing

Nobody will miss the Parmesan cheese in this refreshing, lemony salad! Top with sliced chicken strips, grilled shrimp or salmon for a healthy meal.

Yields: ¾ cup

1 lg. egg yolk

2 garlic cloves, minced

1 whole anchovy, smashed or 1 teaspoon anchovy paste

1 lemon juice and zest

1 Tablespoon Dijon mustard

½ cup extra virgin olive oil

¼ teaspoon Worcestershire sauce

1/8 teaspoon Tabasco or 1/6 teaspoon cayenne pepper

sea salt/freshly ground black pepper

Boil two cups of water in a 2 quart saucepot. Gently lower one egg into the boiling water and set a timer for 1 minute. Take egg out and place in cold water for 1 minute. Crack egg and separate yolk, discard white and shell. Place all ingredients except olive oil into a food processor. Turn on food processor and slowly drizzle olive oil into the pour spout. Turn off processor, taste and adjust seasoning to your liking.

Toss with organic chopped romaine lettuce topped with "parmesan" or spelt croutons (see index)

Vinaigrettes

Homemade salad dressing is so easy, healthy and delicious. It will save you money too!

¼ cup vinegar or citrus juice or ½ cup fruit juice + 1 tablespoon citrus zest

1 tablespoon chopped onion or shallot

1 clove garlic, finely minced (optional)

1 teaspoon agave nectar

1 teaspoon Dijon mustard, organic (don't even think about that yellow stuff for hot dogs only!)

1 tablespoon of fresh chopped herbs (your favorite) or 1 teaspoon dried herbs

2 tablespoons of dried fruit, optional

1 teaspoon sea salt and ½ teaspoon freshly ground black

½ - ¾ cup oil, to your taste* (extra virgin olive oil, grapeseed oil, rice bran oil, sunflower or safflower oil, or nut oil)

Method 1: In a large bowl combine all ingredients except oil, and whisk them together. While vigorously whisking, slowly stream the oil into the bowl to combine. Taste and adjust the seasoning. You can always add a little more vinegar if it is not strong enough. Remember you want to dressing to have a strong flavor because it will be milder when mixed with the salad. If you don't want to whisk: pour everything into a salad dressing cruet or glass jar and shake until combined. Keep in refrigerator for up to one week. Take out 30 minutes before use to let the oil liquefy and shake it up.

Variations:

Balsamic or Red wine vinegar/ Extra Virgin Olive Oil or Grapeseed oil, oregano

Balsamic vinegar, grapeseed oil, dried black mission figs-pureed in a blender

Rice wine vinegar/Rice Bran oil

Champagne vinegar, Rice wine vinegar/ Grapeseed oil

Apple Cider vinegar + Balsamic vinegar/Walnut Oil (omit garlic)

Lime juice/Grapeseed oil, mint or basil

Orange juice/Walnut oil or Grapeseed oil, tarragon or basil

Grapefruit juice/Grapeseed oil, tarragon

Cranberry juice, orange zest/Grapeseed oil or Walnut oil, dried cranberries

Cherry juice, dried cherries/Grapeseed oil

Breakfast

Dutch Baby Pancake

This is baked in the oven and is more like a puffy crepe than a pancake.

Yields: 1 (8-10 inch pancake)-will feed 1-2 people

2 Tablespoons grapeseed or lemon olive oil

½ cup oat flour or barley flour

2 Tablespoons agave nectar or pure maple syrup

½ teaspoon sea salt, fine

½ cup almond milk or light coconut milk

2 lg. organic eggs

lemon, washed and sliced in wedges

vanilla powder, optional

Preheat oven to 375 degrees. Put an 8-10 inch stainless steel sauté pan or cast iron pan into oven and heat for 10 minutes.

Mix all dry ingredients in a large bowl. Measure all wet ingredients and pour into dry ingredients, whisk until combined, set aside. Using pot holders, carefully put 1 Tablespoon into the sauté pan and spread evenly to coat bottom of pan, not the sides. Gently pour the batter into the hot pan and bake for 20-30 minutes or until golden brown and puffy. Serve immediately with lemon wedges and vanilla powder. You can also use maple syrup, agave nectar or fruit spread. Top with fresh sliced strawberries or fresh berries.

Granola

A healthy and tasty granola that you can customize to your own taste! Enjoy with almond or coconut milk or "yogurt" (see index) for breakfast! This will keep you going until lunch!

Yields: approximately 9 cups

4 cups organic rolled oats (not quick cooking) + ½ cup oat bran

2 cups nuts, chopped (walnuts, pecans, almonds, macadamia)

1 ¼ cup shredded coconut, optional

½ cup orange or lemon olive oil or avocado oil or grapeseed oil or nut oil (macadamia, walnut, pecan, pistachio)*

¼ cup agave nectar or 1/3 cup real maple syrup or honey

2 teaspoons real vanilla extract

Zest of 1 lemon or orange

2 teaspoons ground cinnamon, optional

¼ teaspoon freshly grated nutmeg, optional

1 ¼ cup dried fruit (cherries, cranberries, blueberries, apricots, raisins, dates, pineapple etc...)

Preheat oven to 325 degrees. Measure out dried

fruit and set aside. Measure all dry ingredients into a large mixing bowl and stir well. Measure out all wet ingredients into a small bowl and whisk until well combined. Pour wet ingredients over dry ingredients and mix until all liquid is well distributed and absorbed. Pour onto baking sheet and bake on the middle rack of the oven for 10 minutes. Remove from oven and stir in the dried fruit (fruit will burn if you cook it the entire time). Return the granola to the oven and continue to bake for approximately 10-15 more minutes or until golden brown. Be careful and keep a close eye as it burns quickly. Place baking sheet on a cooling rack and cool completely. Store in an airtight jar/container or plastic zip bag at room temperature. I love to keep this at my office for that much needed quick meal!

Please be creative with the flavors and customize it to your own taste. Here are some ideas:

Walnuts and dried cranberries or dates with orange zest, walnut oil or orange olive oil

Pecans and dried apricots with orange zest, lemon olive oil or grapeseed oil

Pecans and dried cherries with lemon zest, orange olive oil

Pistachios and dried blueberries with lemon zest, avocado oil or lemon olive oil

Macadamias, dried pineapple, coconut, orange zest, macadamia oil

For a low fat version: avoid nuts, nut oils and coconut.

Lime "Yogurt"

You'll never miss the dairy in this silky smooth "yogurt". Avocado is the secret ingredient that makes this so healthy! Did you know that Avocado is actually a fruit? Yep! You can find avocado ice cream in South America! This is great for breakfast. Pour over Granola or Muesli and Fruit.

Yields: 2 cups

3 Tablespoons (2 large limes) lime juice

zest of 1 lime

2 Tablespoons agave nectar

½ large Haas avocado

¾ cup regular coconut milk

½ teaspoon Non-GMO soy lecithin granules*, optional

¼ teaspoon real vanilla extract

1/16 teaspoon sea salt, fine

Wash limes with vegetable wash. Zest one lime and juice both limes and put into a blender. Cut avocado in half, cube it with a knife and scoop out flesh with a spoon. Put all ingredients into a blender and blend on low and then high until silky smooth! Can be poured into a glass to drink or eaten from a bowl with a spoon! Enjoy immediately or chill in ramekins for later. Serve alone or pour over granola or add Muesli and fresh cut fruit mix and refrigerate for 4-8 hours.

*Soy lecithin contains high amounts of vitamin B and breaks down stored fat on our bodies. It can be found at a health food store. Keep in the freezer.

Pancakes

As a child I couldn't wait for Saturday mornings as a child because I knew my Dad would make pancakes and there would be no school! There are lots of tasty variations you can use to customize your own pancake-see note below. Kids love to choose their own toppings and put them on the batter themselves-a great way to teach them to cook! This is a nice way to spend a Saturday morning with the people you love creating happy memories.

Yields: 4 servings or 12 pancakes using ¼ cup batter each

1 cup oat or barley flour

¼ cup rye or soy flour

1 Tablespoon baking powder

½ teaspoon sea salt, fine

1/16 teaspoon freshly grated nutmeg, optional

¼ teaspoon ground cinnamon, optional

1-1 ¼ cup almond milk

1 lg. organic egg, beaten

1 teaspoon real vanilla extract

Optional ingredients: peanut butter, almond butter, chocolate chips, banana, pear, berries, coconut, extracts-see note below.

grapeseed oil or vegetable shortening for coating pan

real maple syrup

lemon or orange olive oil or macadamia nut oil (see resources)

Measure all wet ingredients, using 1 cup almond milk to start, and pour into a blender or large bowl. Sift all dry ingredients into wet ingredients and mix just until combined-do not over mix or the pancakes will be tough. If batter is too thick add ¼ cup more of almond milk and stir to combine. For light and fluffy pancakes use a thicker batter, for thin pancakes use a thin batter. Let batter rest for 10 minutes as it will thicken. Heat a flat griddle or cast iron pan or 10 inch sauté pan over medium heat for 2 minutes. Add 1 teaspoon grapeseed oil or vegetable shortening and spread in pan with a paper towel. Drop 1 teaspoon of batter in the middle of the pan, when it sizzles the pan is hot enough. If the pan starts to smoke take it off the heat and return to a low temperature. Pour batter in pan to form circles. Be sure they do not touch and you have enough room to flip them over. You can make them any size you like-sometimes we want one large pancake and sometimes we feel like a stack of smaller ones! If adding any fruit or chocolate chips, place them on top of the batter now. Cook the pancake over medium heat until bubbles come to the top and begin to pop. With a metal spatula, gently flip them over and cook for 2 minutes. Remove from pan and store in a warm oven on a baking sheet or dish. Continue to oil pan before each batch and cooking pancakes until the batter is gone! Heat 2-3 parts real maple syrup and 1 part citrus olive oil or macadamia oil in the microwave or over the stove in a pot until bubbling, about 30 seconds. Pour maple syrup/oil over pancakes and serve immediately. Top with fresh fruit if you like. Pancakes can be kept in the refrigerator or frozen in a plastic freezer zip bag and reheated in the microwave.

Variations:

Peanut butter or Almond butter: whisk ¼ cup almond milk and 2 Tablespoons nut butter until combined. Add to wet ingredients. Use macadamia or walnut oil or orange olive oil.

Banana or pear: wash pears with vegetable wash, rinse well. Slice fruit ¼ inch thick and lay slices over the pancakes after pouring batter into pan. Use lemon olive oil.

Berry (raspberries, blueberries, blackberries, marionberries etc...) - place fresh berries onto batter after pouring into pan-leaving space between the berries. Strawberries are best sliced and put on top of cooked pancakes rather than cooking them.

Chocolate chip: place chocolate chips on top of batter after pouring into pan leaving space between the chocolate chips-use enough to have once chocolate chip per bite-approximately 8 chocolate chips for a 4 inch pancake. Use orange olive oil or macadamia nut oil.

Coconut: add ¼ cup shredded unsweetened coconut+1 teaspoon coconut extract. Use macadamia nut oil. You will feel like you are on tropical vacation eating these!

Mickey Mouse: pour ¼ cup batter into center of the pan, and then pour 1 Tablespoon batter per ear on each side of the top of the pancake. Use berries or chocolate chips for the facial features!

Heart shaped: place a heart shaped cookie cutter in pan and hold it in place. Slowly pour batter into cutter so it completely covers the pan with no gaps. Keep holding the cutter for 30 seconds to 1 minute to let batter set and remove it. You can also try to pour this free form if you are artistically inclined!

Rice flour Pancakes

These are an alternative version of pancakes using rice flour. They are thin and delicious.

Yields: 16 pancakes using ¼ cup batter each

2 cups rice flour, white or brown or red

4 ½ teaspoons baking powder

2 teaspoon agave nectar, optional

2 teaspoon sea salt, fine

2 cups almond milk*

1 lg. organic egg, beaten

1 Tablespoon grapeseed or rice bran oil

oil (grapeseed or citrus olive oil or nut oil)

real maple syrup

Measure all wet ingredients, using 1 cup almond milk to start, and pour into a blender or large bowl. Sift all dry ingredients into wet ingredients and mix just until combined-do not over mix or the pancakes will be tough. If batter is too thick add ¼ cup more of almond milk and stir to combine. For light and fluffy pancakes use a thicker batter, for thin pancakes use a thin batter. Let batter rest for 10 minutes as it will thicken. Heat a flat griddle or cast iron pan or 10 inch sauté pan over medium heat for 2 minutes. Add 1 teaspoon grapeseed oil or vegetable shortening and spread in pan with a paper towel. Drop 1 teaspoon of batter in the middle of the pan, when it sizzles the pan is hot enough. If the pan starts to smoke take it off the heat and return to a low temperature. Pour batter in pan to form circles. Be sure they do not touch and you have enough room to flip them over. You can make them any size you like-sometimes we want one large pancake and sometimes we feel like a stack of smaller ones! Cook the pancake over medium heat until bubbles come to the top and begin to pop. With a metal spatula, gently flip them over and cook for 2 minutes. Remove from pan and store in a warm oven on a baking sheet or dish. Continue to oil pan before each batch and cooking pancakes until the batter is gone! Heat 2-3 parts real maple syrup and 1 part citrus olive oil or macadamia oil in the microwave or over the stove in a pot until bubbling, about 30 seconds. Pour maple syrup/oil over pancakes and serve immediately. Top with fresh fruit if you like. Pancakes can be kept in the refrigerator or frozen in a plastic freezer zip bag and reheated in the microwave.

*rice milk or soy milk may be substituted

Scones

These are a cousin to a biscuit and are served with afternoon tea in England. Often they are topped with lemon curd or raspberry jam, and are delicious with a cup of tea or coffee.

2 ¼ cups oat flour, sifted

3 teaspoons baking powder

½ teaspoon sea salt, fine

1/3 cup vegan Earth Balance or vegetable shortening

1 ½ Tablespoons agave nectar

1 lg. organic egg, beaten

¾ cup almond milk or coconut milk

½ teaspoon pure vanilla extract

½ cup dried cherries or dried fruit of your choice, optional

Zest of 2 tangerines or 1 orange or 1 lemon, optional

One egg white + 1 teaspoon water, beaten

Preheat oven to 400 degrees

Sift all dry ingredients into the bowl of an electric stand mixer. Add Earth Balance and mix with the paddle attachment. Add all wet ingredients, dried fruit, zest and mix just until combined. Scrape out onto a well floured cutting board. Gently roll out to ¾ inch high. Cut into wedges or use a biscuit cutter. Lightly brush the egg white/water mixture over the top of scones. Place on a baking sheet and bake for 15-18 minutes or until golden brown.

Note: Scones are meant to be somewhat dry so they can absorb the lemon curd or Earth Balance and jam that are traditionally served with them. If you want to eat them alone then, bake 2 minutes less.

Let cool on baking sheet for 5 minutes and serve warm. These are best served immediately or the same day. They will get soft and crumbly after one day, especially if it is raining!

Strawberry Smoothie

The sweet flavor of ripe strawberries combined with the creamy texture is divine! Have this for breakfast, a snack or dessert! Delicious anytime!

Yields: 1-2 servings

1 cup fresh or frozen strawberries, washed and hulled

¾ cup coconut milk, light or regular, chilled

2-3 Tablespoons agave nectar

1 tiny pinch sea salt

1 teaspoon real vanilla extract

½ teaspoon Non-GMO soy lecithin, optional*

Put all ingredients into a blender and blend on low speed, holding the top on tightly. Gradually increase the speed to high until smooth. Taste and adjust agave. If it is too thick add more coconut milk. Drink right away while it is cold or chill in the refrigerator.

*Soy lecithin is very high in B vitamins and breaks down stored fats in our bodies!

Beverages

Chai Tea

This is a highly spiced tea that can be sweetened and served with Almond Milk. It is very warming and smells like Christmas time. Very warming on a cold day!

Yields: 6 cups

6 cups filtered or bottled water

20 whole cloves

2-3 star anise

8 whole cardamom pods, broken open

15 whole black peppercorns

4 whole cinnamon sticks

8 slices fresh ginger root, ¼ inch slices

2 Tablespoons black tea, regular or decaf

2-4 Tablespoons agave or honey

1 ½ cups almond milk* (1/4 cup per cup of tea)

Put all spices and water into a 2 quart sauce pot and bring to a boil over high heat. Turn down to a simmer over low heat, cover for 30 minutes. Add tea leaves or bags and steep for 3 minutes. Strain through a sieve into a glass pitcher or large tea pot. Discard spices/tea leaves. Whisk agave or honey into tea. Keep this in the refrigerator for up to 1 week. Add almond milk just before serving or a lemon wedge if you prefer, but not both or it will curdle. Best served hot, but can be chilled.

*Rice or soy milk may be substituted

Chocolate "Milkshake"

Chocolate milkshakes are one of my all time favorite things to drink. What's not to like, the chocolate, the creamy goodness, or how fun it is to decide whether to use a spoon or a straw?

Yields: 1-2 servings

2-3 scoops chocolate or vanilla ice "cream" (see index)

¾-1 cup chilled light coconut milk

2-3 Tablespoons Valrhona cocoa powder

2-3 Tablespoons agave nectar

1 tiny pinch sea salt

1 teaspoon real vanilla extract

½ teaspoon Non-GMO soy lecithin, optional*

Put all ingredients into a blender and blend on low speed, holding the top on tightly. Gradually increase the speed to high until smooth. Taste and adjust agave. If it is too thick add more coconut milk. Drink right away while it is cold or chill in the refrigerator. Serve with a straw and an iced tea spoon! Enjoy!

*Soy lecithin is very high in B vitamins and breaks down stored fats in our bodies! It also helps to emulsify fats and liquids together.

Flavored Water

I try to drink a lot of water and must admit that it gets boring at times. So, I was inspired by some spas that I have visited and saw pitchers of water with various things floating in them! This is my way of adding flavor, without sugar or calories, to my water! I hope it will inspire you to drink more water too! To our health!

Yields: 1 pitcher

1 glass pitcher of bottled or filtered water, sparkling or still

1 bunch fresh organic mint, washed

1 organic cucumber (unpeeled), washed and sliced

1 organic lemon, washed and sliced thinly

1 organic orange, washed and sliced thinly

1 organic lime, washed and sliced thinly

If you cannot find organic fruit and vegetables then wash it with vegetable wash and rinse well to remove pesticides and wax. Place any single or combination or all of the above into a pitcher and add water. Let it sit for at least 2 hours or overnight. I do not recommend using crystal or plastic, glass is the healthiest.

Take it with you in your travel mug. I fill a glass bottle

everyday and keep it in my office. My goal is to drink all of it by the end of the day!

Favorite Combinations:

mint and lemon

mint and lime

lemon and cucumber

lemon, orange and lime

Ginger Lemon Tonic

Ginger has many healthy properties and is warming to the body. I make this when I am under the weather or just need to warm myself up a bit. I also drink it before traveling because it helps reduce motion sickness for me. I am not a doctor and this is not a prescription or cure.

Yields: 1 teapot or approximately 3 cups

4 inch piece of fresh ginger root

4 cups filtered or bottled water

2 Tablespoons honey

juice of 1 lemon

1 bunch lemon thyme, optional

Wash and slice ginger root, with peel on, into 8 slices. Put ginger in a 4 quart saucepot. Add water and bring to a boil. Turn heat down to low and simmer 20 minutes covered. Turn off heat, add honey, lemon and lemon thyme and stir. Cover pot and steep for 15 minutes. Strain through a fine sieve. Return to saucepot and heat to a simmer and serve. This will keep in the refrigerator for 1 week. This can be served cold or hot, but it is best hot.

Hot Chocolate

This is one of the things I really missed most when I stopped eating dairy. After testing many recipes I liked this one the best and hope you will too! My aim was to create a rich and chocolaty drink without sugar or dairy, and I think this is it! See what you think.

Yields: 2 cups, double recipe for 4 cups etc...

4 Tablespoons Valrhona cocoa*

2-4 Tablespoons agave nectar

½ cup regular coconut milk

1 ½ cups unsweetened almond or hazelnut milk* or water

1 teaspoon real vanilla extract, optional

tiny pinch ground cayenne pepper and or ground cinnamon, optional

½ bunch fresh mint (washed), optional

kosher marshmallows, optional

In a saucepot, whisk cocoa, 2 Tablespoons of agave nectar and coconut milk together until smooth. Turn on heat to medium and add the almond milk or water. When it comes to a simmer, turn off the heat. Stir in real vanilla extract. Taste and add 1-2 more

Tablespoons of agave to your taste. Top with kosher marshmallows if you like. Serve immediately.

I don't recommend making this in a microwave oven because it boils over! However, it can be reheated in a microwave, but do it in 30 second intervals and keep a close eye on it.

Variations:

spicy hot chocolate, add cayenne pepper

Mexican hot chocolate: add ground cinnamon or 1 cinnamon stick

Chocolate mint hot chocolate: bring almond milk to a simmer, turn off heat and steep ½ bunch mint in almond milk for 15 minutes.

*I recommend Valrhona cocoa because it is the only cocoa I found that has a deep chocolate flavor and is not bitter. It is worth the extra money.

*Rice or soy milk may be substituted

Ice "Cream" Soda

I remember the first time I had a chocolate egg cream as they are called on the East Coast. I thought this was the most brilliant thing anyone had ever invented! It had ice cream and was fizzy, a kid's dream come true! Not to mention that it came with a straw and iced tea spoon!

Yields: 1 serving! No sharing, unless on a date!

¼ cup regular coconut milk

1/3 cup strawberry puree or chocolate Ganache (see index)

3 Tablespoons agave nectar

1 teaspoon real vanilla extract

1 scoop ice "cream" (vanilla or chocolate or strawberry), see index

½ cup soda or seltzer water

In a tall glass pour coconut milk, strawberry puree or warm chocolate Ganache, agave and vanilla and whisk with a tiny whisk or fork until well combined. Place scoop of ice "cream" on top of the liquid. Tip the glass slightly and SLOWLY pour the soda or seltzer water into the glass, be careful it will fizz up quickly and overflow if you are not careful. Serve immediately with a straw and an iced tea spoon.

Lemonade

This sweet-tart drink is most refreshing on a hot summer day!

Yields: 4 servings

Juice of 4 washed organic lemons

1/3 cup agave nectar or ¼ cup honey*

32 ounces filtered or bottled water, can be still or sparkling, chilled

Wash lemons with vegetable wash and rinse well. Cut lemons in half and squeeze with a lemon juicer into a large pitcher. Whisk in agave. Pour in water and stir well. Taste and adjust the flavor to your own taste by adding more agave or lemon juice. Refrigerate for 2 hours or until cold or use chilled water.

The great things about agave is that first, it melts in cold liquid and second, it has a significantly lower glycemic index than sugar.

*You can use ¼ cup honey instead of agave, but you will need to heat it with the lemon juice to melt it.

Citrus juice can erode the enamel of teeth, so just brush after drinking this wonderful drink!

Limeade

For all you lime lovers out there, here's a delicious sweet and sour thirst quencher!

Yields: 4 glasses

8 whole limes

1/3 cup agave nectar* or ¼ cup honey

32 ounces sparkling water or bottled or filtered water, chilled

Wash limes with vegetable wash and rinse well. Cut limes in half and squeeze with a lemon or lime squeezer/juicer. In a glass pitcher whisk all ingredients together and serve in tall glasses filled with ice. Taste and add more lime juice or agave according to your own taste. Enjoy!

*Agave has a lower glycemic index than sugar or honey. Agave dissolves in cold liquid, and can be served on the side for people to add more if they wish.

I like to chill the water rather than adding ice so it is full strength and doesn't get diluted!

Citrus juice can erode the enamel of teeth, so just brush after drinking this wonderful drink!

Margarita

There is no comparison between a fresh squeezed Margarita and that yellow stuff in a bottle! The taste of sweet orange and sour lemon and lime coupled with tequila makes a satisfying cocktail!

Yields: 1 drink

1 shot gold tequila

1 shot Cointreau or Grand Mariner

juice of ½ orange

juice of 1 lime

juice of ½ lemon

kosher salt for rim, optional

ice cubes

Cut a wedge of citrus and run it along the rim of the glass and dip the rim into kosher salt. Measure all ingredients, except ice, into a cocktail shaker or glass, add ice cubes shake or stir.

Citrus juice can erode the enamel of teeth, so just brush after drinking this wonderful drink!

Cheers!

Mojito

This is a refreshing and delicious Cuban drink that is made with lime, mint and rum.

Yields: 1 drink

6 ounces fresh lime juice

1 Tablespoon agave nectar

10 fresh mint leaves, washed

2 ounces white rum, optional

sparkling water

ice

Wash limes with vegetable wash and rinse well. Squeeze limes in a measuring cup. Remove any seeds with a fork. Pour lime juice into a tall glass. Add mint leaves and muddle (crush with a muddle or wooden spoon) to release essential oils from the mint. Stir in agave nectar. Fill glass with ice. Pour rum in and fill with sparkling water. You can omit the rum for a refreshing alcohol free drink. Enjoy with or without rum. Cheers!

Citrus juice can erode the enamel of teeth, so just brush after drinking this wonderful drink!

Sports Drink

Why buy sports drinks that are filled with unhealthy ingredients when you can make your own? Electrolytes are meant to replace sugar and salt to our bodies. I drink this when I am feeling dehydrated or have a fever or the flu. This is not a prescription or a cure-just my healthy version of a sports drink.

Yields: 48 ounces, 6 (8 ounce) servings

1 32 ounce bottle white or purple grape juice, no sugar added, no preservatives*

1 teaspoon sea salt

¼ cup hibiscus flowers or 3 hibiscus tea bags, optional

2 cups filtered or bottled water

Boil 2 cups water and add sea salt and hibiscus to the hot water. Let hibiscus steep in water for at least 10 minutes. Pour grape juice into a pitcher and stir in hibiscus tea. Chill in the refrigerator. Serve cold or over ice cubes.

*Grape juice concentrate, with no added sugar, and water may be used.

Strawberry "Milkshake"

This takes me back to my childhood and eating out at Diners and ordering a shake! My Dad always said I couldn't have one because I would spoil my appetite, and my Mom said yes! He was right, but what fun is it to eat out and not be able to order a shake? Enjoy!

Yields: 1-2 servings

2-3 scoops strawberry ice "cream" (see index)

¾-1 cup chilled coconut milk, light

½ cup fresh or frozen organic strawberries

1 Tablespoon agave nectar

1 tiny pinch sea salt, fine

1 teaspoon real vanilla extract

½ teaspoon Non-GMO soy lecithin, optional*

Put all ingredients into a blender and blend on low speed, holding the top on tightly. Gradually increase the speed to high until smooth. Taste and adjust agave. If it is too thick add more coconut milk. Drink right away while it is cold or chill in the refrigerator.

*Soy lecithin is very high in B vitamins and breaks down stored fats in our bodies!

Thai Iced Tea

I love this, but find it is way too sweet and has dairy in restaurants. So, here is my sugar free, dairy free version with lots of flavor. Enjoy!

Yields: 8 servings

1 cup Thai tea leaves (available at Asian markets)

8 cups filtered or bottled water

agave nectar, optional

1 can coconut milk, light* or almond milk

lemon slices or lime slices, optional

Bring water to boil in a saucepot and add tea leaves. Steep 5 minutes. Strain through a fine sieve into a tea pot. Whisk in agave nectar to your taste, I like 2-3 teaspoons per 8 ounce glass. Refrigerate until cold. Pour coconut milk or almond milk ¼ way up a tall glass, fill with ice and slowly pour iced tea to fill or add lemon or lime. Do not use lemon or lime if you use coconut milk or it will curdle! You can make this unsweetened and serve the agave on the side for those who would like it. Agave dissolves in cold liquids!

*I prefer coconut milk in this recipe, but rice or soy milk may be substituted.

Be careful, this tea is orange and stains anything it comes in contact with.

Vanilla "Milkshake"

So creamy and smooth with the tropical taste of vanilla!

Yields: 1-2 servings

2-3 scoops vanilla ice "cream" (see index)

¾-1 cup chilled coconut milk, light

2 Tablespoons agave nectar

1 tiny pinch sea salt

2 teaspoons real vanilla extract

½ teaspoon Non-GMO soy lecithin, optional*

Put all ingredients into a blender and blend on low speed, holding the top on tightly. Gradually increase the speed to high until smooth. Taste and adjust agave. If it is too thick add more coconut milk. Drink right away while it is cold or chill in the refrigerator. Serve with a straw and an iced tea spoon! Enjoy!

*Soy lecithin is very high in B vitamins and breaks down stored fats in our bodies! It also helps to emulsify fats and liquids together.

Desserts

Almond Crescents

Crisp on the outside and chewy and soft on the inside with the sweet flavor of almonds!

Yields: 24 cookies

1lbs. (16oz) almond paste*

6 Tablespoons sucanat or date or maple sugar

2 egg whites

sliced almonds

1 cup dark chocolate, melted (optional)

Preheat oven to 350 degrees

In an electric mixer, blend almond paste and sucanat on low speed using paddle attachment. Add whites and mix until smooth. Roll in 1oz portions into logs or make one long roll and cut into 24 even pieces. Roll each piece into a log. Roll in sliced almonds to coat outside. Form into crescents. Bake on parchment or silicone lined baking sheets. Bake for 15 minutes or until golden brown. Cool on a rack.

Optional: dip one end in melted dark chocolate!

*Do not substitute with marzipan

Apple Crisp

Warm soft apples with a crumbly cinnamon laced topping. This is great in the winter during apple season; and much faster than making an apple pie! Serve with vanilla ice "cream".

Yields: 1 (9x12) pan or 2 quart round soufflé dish- serves 6-10 people

Filling:

3 pounds Granny Smith or Fuji apples, 1 inch slices

¾ cup agave nectar for Granny Smith and ½ cup for Fuji

1 teaspoon real vanilla extract

zest and juice of 1 lemon

1 teaspoon tapioca starch or 2 Tablespoons oat or barley flour

Topping:

1 cup oat or barley flour, sifted

½ cup date sugar or maple sugar or sucanat

1 stick vegan Earth Balance, cold or frozen and diced

zest of 1 lemon

1 teaspoon vanilla powder, optional

¼ teaspoon freshly grated nutmeg

¼ teaspoon ground cinnamon

½ cup chopped nuts (walnuts, pecans, almonds)

½ cup old fashioned rolled oats (not quick cooking)

Preheat oven to 350 degrees. Wash lemons and fruit with vegetable wash. Do you know how many people have handled that fruit? Trust me, you don't want to know...just wash it and rinse well with cold water! Slice fruit and put in a large bowl and add the rest of the filling ingredients to the fruit, stir well. Pour into a 9x12 glass baking dish or a 2 quart round soufflé dish or something equivalent-it can be a different shape, but the same size. Set fruit aside. For the topping, place all ingredients into a food processor with the s blade, and pulse until it is crumbly and the size of cherries. Pour evenly over fruit and bake for approximately 30 minutes or until the topping is golden brown and fruit is bubbling. This must be cooled for at least 1 hour.

Topping may be done in a bowl with a pastry cutter if you don't have a food processor.

Apple Pie

The most American dessert with warm apples enveloped in a delicate flaky crust.

Yields: 1 apple pie

2 single piecrusts (1 recipe) see index

12 apples, Granny Smith or McIntosh peeled, cored and sliced ½-1 inch thick*

¾ cup sucanat or ½ cup agave nectar

zest and juice of 1 lemon

1 ½ teaspoons ground cinnamon

 ¼ grated whole nutmeg

1/8 teaspoon ground cloves

2 Tablespoons vegan Earth Balance or vegetable shortening

For top of crust: optional

1 large egg, beaten

2 tablespoons sucanat or maple sugar or date sugar

Roll out one pie crust to ¼ inch thick*. Put it into pie dish and cut the crust along the edge of the pie pan. In a large bowl mix all ingredients except egg and 2 Tablespoons of sucanat. Pour filling into pie shell. Dot with Earth Balance or vegetable shortening. Roll out the other half of pie crust and cut a hole in center of remaining crust with a piping tip or biscuit cutter about 1" in diameter, or cut several vents across top of the pie. Put crust over apple filling. Crimp edges with your clean thumb and fingertips or the ends of a fork to seal the two crusts. Put pie in freezer for ½-1 hour to prevent crust from shrinking. Ten minutes before baking, preheat oven to 375 degrees. Immediately before baking, brush pie with egg and sprinkle with sucanat or maple/date sugar. Bake pie for 1 hour on the second from the bottom shelf of the oven. Bake until crust is golden brown and filling is bubbling. Cool on a wire rack for at least one hour to set the filling. Serve with a scoop of vanilla "ice cream" (see index).

*You can roll the crust on a well floured board or between two pieces of plastic wrap.

* For a chunky pie, slice apples 1 inch thick. For a softer filling, slice apples ½ inch thick.

Berry Crisp

This is my favorite dessert to eat and to share. Frozen fruit is my secret to pretending it is summer in the winter! This is such a delicious treat all year round.

Yields: 1 (9x12) pan or 2 quart round soufflé dish- serves 6-10 people

Filling:

3 pounds of fresh or frozen berries (raspberries, strawberries, blueberries), 1 inch slices

1/3 cup agave nectar

1 teaspoon real vanilla extract

zest and juice of 1 lemon

1 teaspoon tapioca starch or 2 Tablespoons oat or barley flour

Topping:

1 cup oat or barley flour, sifted

½ cup date sugar or maple sugar or sucanat

1 stick vegan Earth Balance, cold or frozen and diced

zest of one lemon

1 teaspoon vanilla powder, optional

¼ teaspoon freshly grated nutmeg

¼ teaspoon ground cinnamon

½ cup chopped nuts (walnuts, pecans, almonds)

½ cup old fashioned rolled oats (not quick cooking)

Preheat oven to 350 degrees. Wash lemons and fruit with vegetable wash. Do you know how many people have handled that fruit? Trust me, you don't want to know...just wash it and rinse well with cold water! Slice fruit and put in a large bowl and add the rest of the filling ingredients to the fruit, stir well. Pour into a 9x12 glass baking dish or a 2 quart round soufflé dish or something equivalent-it can be a different shape, but the same size. Set fruit aside.

For the topping, place all ingredients into a food processor with the s blade, and pulse until it is crumbly and the size of cherries. Pour evenly over fruit and bake for approximately 30 minutes or until the topping is golden brown and fruit is bubbling. This must be cooled for 1 hour.

Topping may be done in a bowl with a pastry cutter if you don't have a food processor.

Buttercream Frosting

This is so light, fluffy and delicious that nobody will miss the butter! I made it for a 3 year old birthday party, and all the kids politely asked for seconds! I couldn't have received a higher compliment than that one! All the parents loved that there was Agave instead of sugar, and the kids didn't know the difference! Have your cake and frosting with no sugar highs and lows!

Yields: 2 ¼ cups

1 lg. organic egg

5 lg. organic egg yolks

1 cup agave nectar

1 stick vegan Earth Balance, chilled and cubed

1 teaspoon real vanilla extract

Place egg and yolks into the bowl of an electric mixer and whip with whisk on medium high speed for 7 minutes then, turn on low and keep it mixing. While eggs are mixing, pour the agave into a 1 quart saucepot. Place a candy thermometer attached to the side of the saucepot so it is not touching the bottom of the pot, but is in the agave. Over medium high heat and bring the agave to 250 degrees. With mixer still mixing on low speed, slowly pour the agave between the whisk and edge of the bowl, being careful not to pour it onto the whisk as it will splatter. Turn up to medium high speed and mix for 5 minutes, until the outside of the bowl is warm not hot. With the mixer on medium high speed add one cube of vegan Earth Balance at a time and beat until smooth and shiny, about 15 minutes. Add real vanilla extract or any other extract you may desire and mix on medium high speed for 2 more minutes. Frost cake immediately with an offset spatula or refrigerate for up to 4 days in a plastic or glass container. Buttercream may be frozen in a plastic or glass container. If frozen defrost to room temperature. It easiest to spread at room temperature.

Cheesecake

So velvety smooth and creamy nobody will be able to distinguish it from the traditional version!

Yields: 1 cheesecake (10 inches)

1 ½ cups cookie crumbs*

¾ cup pecans or walnuts or hazelnuts, chopped (optional-can use ¾ cup cookie crumbs instead)

3 Tablespoons sucanat or maple or date sugar

½ stick vegan Earth Balance or vegetable margarine, melted and cooled

24 oz. soy cream cheese

1 cup agave nectar

3 lg. organic eggs

3/4 cup regular coconut milk or plain soy yogurt

2 teaspoons real vanilla extract

1 Tablespoon lemon zest, optional, but highly recommended

1/8 teaspoon sea salt, fine

Preheat oven to 350 degrees.

Melt and cool Earth Balance to room temperature. In food processor, with the s blade, process pecans until finely chopped, put in a bowl and set aside. Process cookie crumbs until they are a fine crumb, pour into nuts. Add sucanat and melted Earth Balance to nut mixture and stir until well combined. Pour into springform pan and press it down on bottom and half way up the sides. Set aside.

In an electric stand mixer, with the paddle attachment, mix soy cream cheese and agave until smooth and creamy. Scrape down the sides and bottom of bowl and continue to mix. Add eggs, one at a time and mix. Add all the rest of the ingredients and mix until smooth. Gently pour into the springform pan. Tap on counter to release air bubbles. Put on a baking sheet and bake on the middle rack for 50 minutes. Remove from oven and cool on a rack to room temperature. Chill overnight or at least 4 hours in the refrigerator. Top with fruit and/or serve with fruit sauce (see index).

* Use one of the following cookie recipes: double chocolate chip, ginger, chocolate chip or pecan sandies (see index).

Chocolate Cake

My all time favorite cake! My Mom always baked a chocolate cake with chocolate frosting for my birthday, and I could not wait to eat it! Here's a much healthier version of that sugary cake from a box and a can-sorry Mom! The perfect children's birthday cake! Vegan friendly too!

Yields: 1 (9x13) cake or two 8 inch round cakes

3 cups oat flour

½ cup Valrhona cocoa powder

2 teaspoons baking soda

2 teaspoons baking powder

1 teaspoon sea salt, fine

½ cup grapeseed oil

½ cup real maple syrup

¾ cup agave nectar

2 cups coconut milk or unsweetened almond milk

2 teaspoons apple cider vinegar

1 teaspoon real vanilla extract or 1 vanilla bean

Preheat oven to 350 degrees. Oil pan with vegan Earth Balance or grapeseed oil, then dust with oat flour and tap out any excess. Sift all dry ingredients into the bowl of an electric stand mixer. Measure out all liquid ingredients and add to dry ingredients. If using vanilla beans, cut in half lengthwise and scrape out seeds with the back of a knife. Whisk the vanilla bean seeds into the wet ingredients. Either discard vanilla bean or put it into a jar of sucanat for flavor. Place paddle attachment onto mixer and mix on low speed just until incorporated. Stop mixer and scrape down sides and bottom of the bowl, mix briefly until smooth. Pour batter into cake pan and bake on the middle rack of oven for 40 minutes. Insert a toothpick in the middle of the cake and it is done when it comes out clean. If it does not come out clean continue baking approximately 5 more minutes and continue to check with a toothpick until it comes out clean. Cool on a rack until completely cool. Remove from round pans. You can keep it in the 9x13 pan. Frost with "Buttercream" or Ganache (see index). This cake can be double wrapped in plastic and then put into a freezer plastic zip bag and frozen for up to one month.

Chocolate Chip Cookies

These have a delicate cakey texture and are different from the traditional ones, but they taste just as good!

Yields: 24 cookies

2 sticks vegan Earth Balance or 1 cup vegetable shortening, room temperature

1 cup pure maple syrup

½ cup sucanat or agave nectar

1 teaspoon real vanilla extract

2 organic lg. eggs

2 ¼ cups oat flour

1 teaspoon baking soda

2 cups chocolate chips, non-dairy

1 cup chopped walnuts, optional

Preheat oven to 350 degrees

In an electric mixer, cream the Earth Balance, maple syrup and agave or sucanat, until light and fluffy with the paddle attachment. Add eggs one at a time and mix until incorporated. Add vanilla extract. Sift together all dry ingredients into a bowl and mix into egg/sugar mixture on low speed. Stir in chocolate chips and nuts. Dip a 1 Tbsp. ice cream scooper or measuring spoon into cookie dough and place them onto a cookie sheet. Use a cup of very hot water to dip the scooper in between cookies so dough does not stick. Bake for 12 minutes. Remove from oven and let cool for 5 minutes on the baking sheet then remove cookies from pan with a spatula onto a wire cooling rack.

Chocolate Cupcakes

Chocolate can brighten you up no matter what is happening at that moment! Great for traveling or when you want an individual dessert neatly wrapped in its own packaging. Kids love this at parties! Adults can eat this small portion with much less guilt than a large piece of cake!

Yields: 24 cupcakes, regular size

3 cups oat flour

½ cup Valrhona cocoa powder

2 teaspoons baking soda

2 teaspoons baking powder

1 teaspoon sea salt, fine

½ cup grapeseed oil

½ cup real maple syrup or agave nectar

¾ cup agave nectar

2 cups coconut milk or unsweetened almond milk*

2 teaspoons apple cider vinegar

1 teaspoon real vanilla extract or 1 vanilla bean

1 teaspoon instant espresso powder, optional

Preheat oven to 350 degrees. Oil pan with vegan Earth Balance or grapeseed oil or place paper liners into cups. Sift all dry ingredients into the bowl of an electric stand mixer. Measure out all liquid ingredients, set aside. If using vanilla beans, cut in half lengthwise and scrape out seeds with the back of a knife. Whisk the vanilla bean into the wet ingredients to evenly distribute the seeds. Add wet ingredients to dry ingredients. Place paddle attachment onto mixer and mix on low speed just until incorporated. Stop mixer and scrape down sides and bottom of the bowl, mix briefly until smooth. Pour batter into cupcake pan or liners filling ¾ of the way to the top. Place muffin pan on a baking sheet. Bake on the middle rack of oven for 20-30 minutes. Insert a toothpick in the middle of the cupcake and it is done when it comes out clean. If it does not come out clean continue baking approximately 5 more minutes and continue to test. Cool on a rack until completely cool. Frost with "buttercream" or Ganache (see index). Decorate with fresh berries or whatever you like.

For transporting place cupcakes back into a clean cupcake pan or disposable cups. Insert a toothpick into all four cupcakes in each corner and one in the center so they are sticking up ¾ of the way out the top. Gently cover with foil, put into a large shopping bag with handles and place on the floor of your car and take it slowly around those corners! Trust me on the driving tip!

*Rice milk may be substituted

Chocolate Fondue

Nothing says "party" more than a chocolate fondue! This is a wonderful dessert and a fun way to serve a quick and healthy dessert or get your kids to eat more fruit! It's really fun for big kids too (adults)!

Yields: plenty for a party using 3 cups Ganache

1 fondue pot

fondue forks and/or bamboo skewers

1 recipe chocolate Ganache using good dark chocolate*, (see index)

1 large platter of fresh fruits washed and cut into ½ inch chunks such as: whole stemmed organic strawberries, pineapple, honeydew melon and cantaloupe (scoop rounds with melon baller), whole seedless grapes and mango. Apples and bananas are not the best choice because they turn brown, but you can toss them with fresh lemon or lime juice to prevent or slow browning. Small berries tend to fall off the forks/sticks into the fondue. Dried fruit is too sweet. If you really want to do this in the winter, you can use frozen fruit, but the fresh fruit texture is far superior.

Yellow cake cubes, 1 inch (see index)

1-2 Bags large kosher marshmallows, optional

*Valrhona, Callebaut, Dagoba, Green and Blacks
with approximately 70% cocoa

Chocolate Ganache

This is the most versatile sauce. It can be used for an ice "cream" topping, dessert sauce, frosting and truffles. It is thick and fudgy when it is cold and thin and syrupy when it is warm. What's not to like about that? Absolutely nothing! Shh, it's great to just scoop out of the jar when it's cold for that sweet tooth fix! Ganache is simply equal parts of chocolate and cream, but we will use coconut milk instead of cream.

Yields: 3 cups-enough to frost one 9x12 cake or double layer 8 inch round cake or 3 dozen cupcakes

12 ounces dark chocolate (Valrhona, Callebaut, Dagoba, Green and Blacks) or chocolate chips**

1 ½ cups regular coconut milk (not light)

½ cup Valrhona cocoa powder, optional but recommended!

*For sweeter frosting you can add ¼ cup agave nectar to the coconut milk, optional

Place chocolate in a metal or glass bowl and set aside. Put coconut milk in a saucepot and bring to a boil, pour over chopped chocolate. See note for sweeter frosting above-if using chocolate chips it will be sweet enough. Let it sit for 1-2 minutes and then stir with a silicone spatula until smooth and well mixed.

For a shiny glaze over cake: pour directly over cake and let it set at room temperature for a few hours- do not refrigerate. Best when the cake is in a pan. If you are doing it over a round cake on a stand, pour half over it and let it set and then pour the other half so it doesn't all run to bottom of the cake onto the stand and not on your cake!

For a fluffy frosting: Chill the Ganache in the refrigerator until it is completely set and thick like fudge. Put into an electric stand mixer, fitted with the paddle attachment, and mix on medium-high speed until it is fluffy. For a really deep, dark chocolate flavor, add ½ cup Valrhona cocoa powder, and mix on low speed until smooth and completely incorporated. For sweeter frosting you can add ¼ cup agave nectar to the coconut milk, optional. The amount of agave will depend on the bitterness of the chocolate that is used. Spread onto the cake and leave at room temperature or refrigerate to use later.

For chocolate sauce or topping: use warm. Let Ganache cool to room temperature and then store it in a glass jar or container with a lid in the refrigerator. Never put warm or hot food directly into any plastic as it releases toxins that can be absorbed into your food. Spoon out the amount you need and heat on low over stove, stirring constantly so it does not burn or microwave in 10 second intervals, stirring in between-it can burn in the microwave too.

Wonderful over ice "cream" or alongside cake or over fresh fruit or berries. See the ice "cream" soda recipe too. You can put this into a fondue pot and keep it warm and serve a platter of fruit and cut up cake cubes to dip in the chocolate fondue (see index).

**Be sure the chocolate chips are dairy free

Chocolate Molten Lava Cakes

The center of these little cakes is a heavenly, thick chocolate sauce that runs out when cut into. This is a quick and very popular dessert. Great with vanilla ice "cream" (see index) or a cup of coffee, tea or liqueur.

Yields: 6 individual cakes

12 ounces chopped dark chocolate (Valrhona, Callebaut, Dagoba, Green and Blacks) 72% cocoa

¼ cup vegan Earth Balance

1/3 cup agave nectar or ½ cup sucanat or date sugar or maple sugar

4 lg. organic eggs, beaten

1 teaspoon real vanilla extract

1/3 cup oat or barley flour

Preheat oven to 400 degrees. Grease 6 ceramic ramekins with vegan Earth Balance, set aside. Melt chopped chocolate over a double boiler with water simmering. Stir chocolate until smooth and set aside off of the heat and cool to room temperature. In an electric stand mixer, with paddle attachment, mix vegan Earth Balance and agave or sugar together until light and fluffy on medium low speed. Add eggs slowly while mixer is on low speed. Add vanilla and mix until well incorporated. Pour cooled chocolate into egg mixture and mix on low speed until smooth. Sift flour into the mixer and mix on low just until it is incorporated-don't over mix or the cake will be tough. Immediately pour batter into 6 ceramic ramekins and bake on a baking sheet for 6-8 minutes. They are done when they are set around the edges and still soft but wobbly (like a cheesecake) in the center. Using a pot holder, carefully invert them onto a plate and add a scoop of vanilla ice "cream" or raspberry sauce. Eat immediately or they will set and the center and will not run out like lava. A glass of your favorite liqueur such as Frangelico, Amaretto, Chambord, Cognac, or a cup of coffee or tea is a nice compliment to these heavenly delicious little cakes.

Chocolate Mousse

I know the French will not believe you can make this without cream, but I have and it is delicious with fewer calories than the traditional version! I think even Julia Child would be pleasantly surprised! As a child, chocolate mousse meant it was a special occasion! A quick and easy dessert to prepare; with a light and airy texture and has the flavor of rich, deep, dark chocolate!

Yields: 1 large bowl or 4 servings

4 ounces high quality 72% dark chocolate (Valrhona, Callebaut, Swiss, South American)

5 lg. organic egg yolks

¼ cup agave nectar

1 cup pasteurized egg whites (fresh or Eggology), organic at room temperature*

1 Tablespoon liquor (Grand Mariner, Chambord, Cognac etc...), optional

1 teaspoon real vanilla extract

Separate eggs, reserve 5 egg yolks for later. Add water to the bottom of a double boiler or a sauce pot fitted with a glass or metal bowl on top, and bring water to a simmer over high heat. Turn heat to low when it is simmering. Chop chocolate into small pieces the size of chocolate chips. Place chocolate in the top of the double boiler or bowl and let it melt. Stir the chocolate until completely melted and then remove from heat and let cool to room temperature. In a very clean and dry bowl of an electric mixer, place egg whites and whip on medium high with whisk attachment to a stiff peak, but not dry. A stiff peak is when you remove the whisk and the egg whites will form a peak without falling when you hold the whisk with the end up and the top in your hand. Gently pour whites into another, clean and dry, bowl and set aside. Place yolks and agave in an electric mixer and whip on medium high with the whisk attachment until pale and fluffy, about 2 minutes. Slowly pour the cooled chocolate into the yolk mixture and mix until combine with no streaks. Pour in liquor and vanilla extract into the yolks and stir until incorporated. Remove whisk and stir in ¼ of the whites to soften the mixture. Gently fold the rest of the whites into the yolks with a rubber or silicone spatula. Spoon the chocolate mousse into a large glass or ceramic serving bowl and serve family style or spoon into four individual glass or crystal goblets. If you are feeling artistic, pipe the mousse with a piping bag fitted with a large star tip. Chill for 4 -8 hours or until set/firm. This is best made the day you will serve it as the whites will separate with time. Top with fresh berries and shaved chocolate and enjoy without guilt. Bon Appetite!

*Bring eggs to room temperature by placing them

in a bowl of very warm to hot tap water until they don't feel cold to the touch.

*You can use an electric hand mixer for this recipe. I don't recommend whipping it by hand unless you want a really good workout! Pasteurized eggs are safer since the eggs are not being cooked which kills the bacteria.

Chocolate Truffles

These will melt in your mouth and transport you to a place in your dreams! Whether they are pure chocolate or minty, spicy, exotic, fruity, or have a touch of espresso they are decadent!

Yields: approximately 30 truffles

5 ounces of dark chocolate 72% (Valrhona, Callebaut, Dagoba, Green and Blacks), chopped

1/3 cup regular coconut milk (don't use light)

2 Tablespoons Tupelo honey (must be tupelo)*

1/16 teaspoon fine sea salt

1 Tablespoon liquor (rum, brandy, Grand Mariner, Chambord, Frangelico, Amaretto, Kahlua), optional

Optional spices (choose one of the combinations below):

¼ teaspoon ground chipotle powder + 1/8 teaspoon ground cinnamon

1/8 teaspoon freshly grated nutmeg + 1 Tablespoon real vanilla extract

2 Tablespoons raspberry jam

1 teaspoon earl gray tea

1 teaspoon instant espresso powder

½ bunch fresh spearmint leaves*

Dipping:

5 ounces of dark chocolate 72% (Valrhona, Callebaut, Dagoba, Green and Blacks), chopped

2 cups Valrhona cocoa powder

1 cup finely chopped nuts (walnuts, almonds, pecans, peanuts), optional

Place 5 ounces of dark chocolate in a metal or glass bowl and set aside. In a saucepot, bring coconut milk and honey to a boil and pour over chocolate. For tea truffles: use earl gray tea steep in hot coconut milk for 3 minutes and strain. For chocolate mint truffles: use spearmint and steep the leaves in the hot coconut milk for 20 minutes and strain. For mocha truffles: use espresso powder and whisk it into the hot coconut milk. Bring the coconut milk and honey to a boil and then add to chocolate. Let it sit for 1-2 minutes and then stir with a spatula scraping the sides and bottom of the bowl until smooth. Stir in liquor, spices or jam-you can divide the truffle mixture into 2-3 equal portions for different flavors. Refrigerate chocolate filling until set-approximately 1 hour. When the chocolate is firm all the way through, and the consistency of fudge, remove from refrigerator. Get out a baking sheet and line with parchment. Place cocoa powder in a rectangular backing dish such as a 9x9 inch glass dish and set next to the baking sheet. If using nuts place them in a 9x9 baking dish and set between the melted chocolate and the baking sheet. Melt 5 ounces of chocolate in a double boiler or in a glass or metal bowl over simmering water. Keep the water simmering for later. Using a 1 oz metal ice cream scooper, scoop the chocolate filling and drop into the melted chocolate roll around with a chocolate dipping fork until well coated. Dip the scooper into very hot water occasionally if it gets too gooey and dry it completely. Water is an enemy of chocolate and will make it seize and destroy the texture. Lift the truffle out of the melted chocolate and gently put it into the cocoa powder. If you don't like cocoa powder then just set the truffle on the baking sheet to set or roll in the chopped nuts. Otherwise, let the truffles sit in the cocoa powder until the pan is full. If the melted chocolate gets too thick just put is over the simmering water and melt it again and stir it until it is smooth. Let truffles set at room temperature until chocolate has set. Keep in an airtight container at room temperature. These make a great gift, put into a clean Chinese take-out container or plastic decorator bag and tie a ribbon around it! Indulge and enjoy!

Coffee "Ice Cream"

This is for the true coffee lovers! The combination of the creaminess and coffee flavor is a match made in heaven or maybe Italy!

Yields: 1 quart

Special Equipment: Ice cream maker or Kitchen Aid frozen ice cream bowl attachment with paddle

2 cups regular coconut milk*

1 ½ cups light coconut milk, chilled

6 Tbsp. instant espresso*

3/4 cup clover honey or agave nectar*

6 lg. organic egg yolks

In a saucepan, heat 1 2/3 cup regular coconut milk, ½ cup agave nectar or honey and espresso powder over medium-high heat until it simmers (170 degrees). In an electric mixer, with whisk attachment, beat egg yolks on medium-high or speed 6 about 5 minutes until pale and light and a thick ribbon runs off the whisk when lifted. Reduce to low speed and slowly drizzle in 1 cup of hot coconut milk/honey or agave.

Pour egg/coconut milk mixture back into saucepan of the remaining coconut milk. Whisk constantly over medium-high heat until it is thick and at 180 degrees. Dip a spoon into mixture and wipe a clean line across the middle of the spoon. If the line stays clean and the mixture does not run down into the line, it's done, otherwise continue to cook a little longer and test every minute. If you overcook it, it will curdle. Add remaining chilled light coconut milk. Cover mixture and refrigerate 6 hours or until 38 degrees. Be sure you have a thermometer in your refrigerator and keep it between 34-38 degrees-over 40 degrees is optimal temperature for bacterial growth!

Follow the manufacturer's ice cream machine instructions to churn. When finished churning, pour into plastic containers and freeze for 8 hours or overnight for premium ice cream texture, or eat a little of it now, which will be soft serve consistency. Scoop and enjoy!

*Note: you can use all light coconut milk, but the texture will not be as creamy. You can use instant coffee instead of espresso, but the flavor will not be as pronounced. Honey is sweeter than agave.

Cream Puffs

This dough is also called Pate a Choux. One of my favorite desserts that I thought I would never be able to enjoy again, until now! A delicate cream puff shell filled with vanilla pastry cream topped with dark chocolate Ganache! Heaven! This was inspired by my favorite pastry chef Jacques Torres who writes the best recipes and directions I've ever seen-many thanks. I visited Le Cirque restaurant in New York and Jacques most generously sent out 11 full sized desserts to my table (when I requested a sampler platter) and everyone wondered who I was...! That was one of the best nights of my life and I will never forget it! Merci Beaucoup Jacques!

Yields: approximately 20 (2 inch) cream puffs

1 ¼ cups filtered or bottled water

1 teaspoon agave nectar

½ cup + 1 Tablespoon vegan Earth Balance

1 ¼ cups oat flour

5 lg. organic whole eggs (using large eggs is very important)

1 recipe pastry cream (see index)

1 recipe chocolate Ganache, cooled to room temperature and slightly thick (see index)

Preheat oven to 400 degrees. Put water, agave and

vegan Earth Balance in a 4 quart sauce pot and bring to a boil over medium high heat. Remove from heat and add all of the flour at once. Stir well with a strong wooden spoon. Return to stove over medium heat and stir constantly for 3 minutes-a great workout for the arms! Be sure to turn it over a few times. It is done after 3 minutes and a film is on the bottom of the pot. Pour pate a choux into an electric mixer fitted with the paddle attachment and beat on low speed for 2 minutes to cool so the eggs will not scramble. Turn mixer to medium speed and add one egg at a time and mix until well incorporated. Don't worry if it separates as it will come back together after all eggs are added. With a silicone spatula scoop dough into a piping bag, fitted with ½ inch round tip, fill ¾ full. Scrape dough to bottom and twist the top of the bag closed. Gently squeeze onto a baking sheet into 2 inch circles. Hold the tip in place and squeeze until it is 2 inches at the base then, stop squeezing and pull up to form a tip. Twelve cream puffs will fit onto one baking sheet-three across and four rows down. Only pipe 12 and save the rest for a second batch as they need to bake on the middle rack of the oven. Wet your fingers and gently push the tip top of the circles flat. Bake at 400 degrees for 15 minutes, and then 15 more minutes at 350 degrees. While baking first batch, pipe the second batch the same way as the first. Remove first batch and cool completely. Turn the oven back up to 400 and bake second pan for 15 minutes, turn down to 350 degrees and bake 15 more minutes. Remove from oven and cool completely. Wash and dry the pastry bag and tip, fill ¾ of the way with pastry cream. Poke a hole in the bottom of the cream puff shell with the pastry tip and squeeze bag to fill. Dip tops into chocolate Ganache. Let the chocolate set/firm up at room temperature. They can be refrigerated, but are best at room temperature. DO NOT FREEZE pastry cream or chocolate. Serve and enjoy!

Dark Chocolate "Ice Cream"

My sister gave me the highest compliment when she tasted this by saying that it was as good as the number one premium ice cream! I hope you think so too. The secret is using a very high quality chocolate. This one is for you Mary Clo!

Yields: 1 quart

Special Equipment: Ice cream maker or Kitchen Aid frozen ice cream bowl attachment with paddle, glass pitcher.

2 cups regular coconut milk*

1 ½ cups light coconut milk, chilled

1/3 cup organic Valrhona cocoa powder

6 oz. dark chocolate (70 %+), finely chopped**

½ cup agave nectar or clover honey

6 lg. organic egg yolks

1 tsp. real vanilla extract

In a saucepan, heat 1 2/3 cup regular coconut milk, ½ cup agave nectar or honey over medium-high heat until it simmers (170 degrees). Sift in 1/3 cup cocoa powder and whisk.

In an electric mixer, with whisk attachment, beat egg yolks on medium-high or speed 6 about 5 minutes until pale and light and a thick ribbon runs off the whisk when lifted. Reduce to low speed 2 and slowly drizzle in 1 cup of hot coconut milk/honey or agave.

Pour egg/coconut milk mixture back into saucepan of the remaining coconut milk. Whisk constantly over medium-high heat until it is thick and at 180 degrees. Dip a spoon into mixture and wipe a clean line across the middle of the spoon. If the line stays clean and the mixture does not run down into the line, it's done, otherwise continue to cook a little longer and test every minute. If you overcook it, it will curdle. Remove from heat and pour in chopped chocolate, let sit 1 minute and whisk until smooth. Add remaining chilled light coconut milk, 1 teaspoon real vanilla extract and whisk. Pour into a glass pitcher, cover mixture and refrigerate 6 hours or until 38 degrees. Be sure you have a thermometer in your refrigerator and keep it between 34-38 degrees-over 40 degrees is optimal temperature for bacterial growth!

Follow the manufacturer's ice cream machine instructions to churn. When finished churning, pour into plastic containers and freeze for 8 hours or overnight for premium ice cream texture, or eat a little of it now, which will be soft serve consistency. Scoop and enjoy!

*Note: you can use all light coconut milk, but the texture will not be as creamy.

**I recommend Valrhona, Dagoba, Callebaut or a combination.

Honey is sweeter than agave.

Dark Chocolate Pudding

What is more satisfying than creamy, smooth dark chocolate pudding? A favorite of small and big kids! It's a real bowl licker!

Yields: 6 (½ cup servings)

6 lg. organic egg yolks

½ cup agave nectar or ¾ cup sucanat or date sugar or maple sugar

¼ cup tapioca starch or cornstarch

¼ cup Valrhona cocoa powder

Pinch of sea salt, fine

2 cups coconut milk, regular

2 oz. bittersweet or 72% dark chocolate, chopped (Valrhona, Callebaut, Dagoba)

1 teaspoon real vanilla extract

In the bowl of an electric mixer, with the paddle attachment beat the egg yolks and sucanat on medium-high speed until thick and fluffy, approximately 3 minutes. Sift the tapioca starch, cocoa and salt into the egg mixture, mix thoroughly on low speed. Pour the coconut milk into a saucepan and bring to a simmer over medium-low heat, keep a close eye so it doesn't boil over. Turn the mixer on low speed and slowly pour the hot coconut milk into the egg mixture until it is blended. Pour the mixture back into the saucepan and whisk constantly over low heat for 2 minutes. Remove from heat and whisk in chopped chocolate until melted. Cool for 5 minutes and then whisk in vanilla extract. Ladle or spoon the pudding into small bowls or ramekins. Cover with plastic wrap and refrigerate until set, about 2 hours. If you like a "skin" on the pudding then just cover it with plastic wrap that is not touching the pudding. If you do not like a "skin", place the plastic wrap directly on top of the surface of the pudding. Pudding can be eaten warm too! It will thicken as it cools and is worth the wait!

Double Chocolate Chip Cookies

These rich chocolaty cookies are crisp on the outside and chewy on the inside, and taste like Brownies!

Yields: 24 cookies

¼ cup grapeseed oil

3/4 cup pure maple syrup or agave or honey

½ cup sucanat or agave*

1 teaspoon real vanilla extract

1 ¾ cups oat flour

½ cup unsweetened cocoa powder*

½ teaspoon baking powder

½ teaspoon sea salt, finely ground

1 cup chocolate chips, non-dairy

1 cup chopped walnuts, optional

Preheat oven to 350 degrees

In an electric mixer, with the paddle attachment, add oil, maple syrup, sucanat or agave and vanilla extract, mix on low-medium speed until ingredients are combined. Sift together all dry ingredients into a bowl and to wet ingredients in electric mixer on low speed just until combined. Stir in chocolate chips and nuts. Dip a Tbsp. ice cream scooper or measuring spoon into cookie dough and place them onto a silpat or greased cookie sheet. Use a cup of very hot water to dip the scooper in so dough does not stick. Dip the bottom of drinking glass in water and gently press down on the top of the cookies to flatten the tops. Bake for 12 minutes. Remove from oven and let cool for 5 minutes then remove cookies from pan with a spatula onto a cooling rack.

*Use a premium cocoa such as Valrhona

*use sucanat for best chewy texture

English Sherry Trifle

I had this dessert while visiting Oxford, England many years ago and fell in love with it. The friends I was staying with were invited to a party and needed to make a quick dessert and this is what they made! What a brilliant idea for a quick and satisfying dessert. Trifle has soft cake soaked in sherry with fruity jam and creamy pudding topped with fresh berries and crunchy toasted almonds. Simply scrumptious!

Yields: 4-6 servings

½ yellow cake recipe, 1 inch cubes (see index)

¼ cup dry sherry*

½ cup raspberry or strawberry fruit spread or jam

1 recipe vanilla pudding (see index)

1 pint each: fresh raspberries, blueberries or blackberries, strawberries (quartered) *

½ cup sliced almonds, toasted

Make cake and vanilla pudding and set aside to cool to room temperature. Wash and dry the strawberries, quarter them and set aside. Dice the cake into 1 inch cubes and put on the bottom of a large glass or crystal bowl. Drizzle sherry over the cake evenly. Spread the fruit spread evenly on top of the cake. Pour the vanilla pudding at room temperature over the cake. Evenly sprinkle the berries and almonds over the top. Chill for 1 hour if you have time or serve immediately. This is so great to take to a party or to whip up for a quick last minute dessert. Everyone will love it. Enjoy!

*Sherry can be omitted, but it really will not be the same. Frozen berries can be used in a pinch, but the texture and appearance is not ideal. Strawberries will bleed so put them on just before serving.

Flourless Decadence Chocolate Cake

A food critic once wrote that this heavenly cake had wings! It is very dense and fudgy, and for chocoholics. Great served with raspberry sauce and fresh raspberries and/or vanilla ice "cream" (see index). This was my signature cake when I was a Pastry Chef with the secret ingredients of cinnamon and cayenne pepper. Enjoy!

Yields: 1 (10 inch round cake)

12 ounces dark chocolate* 72% (Valrhona, Callebaut, Dagoba), chopped

¾ cup agave nectar

6 lg. organic eggs

¼ cup agave nectar

1 teaspoon real vanilla extract

¼ teaspoon ground cinnamon, optional

1/8 teaspoon ground ancho chile powder or cayenne pepper, optional

Line a 10 inch round cake pan with parchment. Do not butter it or it will stick! Preheat oven to 350 degrees. Boil ¾ cup agave, remove from heat and add chopped chocolate. Let it sit for 1-2 minutes and then stir with a silicone spatula until chocolate is dissolved and set aside.

In an electric stand mixer, with paddle attachment, beat eggs and ¼ cup agave nectar until light and fluffy, approximately 2 minutes. Add vanilla extract, cinnamon and chile then, mix until well combined. Pour chocolate mixture into egg mixture and mix on low speed until mixed well. Pour batter into 10 inch pan. Bake on the center rack of the oven for 1 hour and 15 minutes. Do not use a convection oven. The cake will crack; don't panic as it will settle after cooling. Cool on a wire rack at room temperature for 1 hour. Transfer to refrigerator and cool on a rack for 8 hours or overnight. Do not cover until it is completely cool or the water will form and drip on it.

When you are ready to unmold it, run a sharp paring knife around the edge of the cake alongside the pan twice making sure the knife is all the way to the bottom of the pan. Place the cake pan over a very low flame/heat of the stove for 30 seconds or just until it will twist around. Take your clean hand and place it on top of the cake and turn it-when it turns it's done. Put a plate over the pan and invert it. You should feel or hear it drop. If not, just give it a few pats on the bottom of the pan. Cut into 10-12 pieces-it is very rich. For a match made in Heaven, serve with raspberry sauce, fresh raspberries and or vanilla ice "cream" (see index).

If you happen to have leftover cake, wrap in plastic wrap and then refrigerate it or freeze it in a plastic zip bag.

*You must use high quality chocolate if you want great flavor-this is not the time to be frugal!

Fudgy Brownies

These are very fudgy, but if you like cakey brownies see note.

Yields: One 9x9 pan or 9 brownies

6 Tbsp. (3/4 stick) vegan Earth Balance, cubed

2 c. chopped 60% dark chocolate (Valrhona, Callebaut, Dagoba) or chocolate chips

1 c. semisweet chocolate chips*

2 lg. organic eggs

½ c. honey or agave nectar OR 1 c. sucanat

1 ½ tsp. real vanilla extract

½ c. oat flour

¼ tsp. baking powder

1 Tbsp. Valrhona cocoa powder **

1/8 tsp. ground cinnamon, optional

1 c. chopped nuts (walnuts, pecans, macadamia, hazelnuts), optional

For an exotic flavor combination: add 1/8 tsp. ground cayenne pepper OR 1/8 tsp. ground cardamom, optional

Preheat oven to 350 degrees

Grease and flour a 9x9 inch square baking dish (preferably glass).

Fill saucepan or double boiler ½ the way up with hot water, bring to a simmer. Place 2 cups chocolate and Earth Balance in a heat proof bowl, or insert of double boiler, melt over simmering water stir occasionally. When there are a few unmelted pieces of chocolate, remove from heat and stir. Set aside and let it cool to room temperature.

In a bowl of an electric mixer, fitted with a whisk attachment on medium high speed beat eggs and agave or honey or sucanat until fluffy, approximately 3-4 minutes. Add the vanilla extract and mix. Stir in one cup of egg mixture into the chocolate mixture to lighten it. Replace the whisk attachment with the paddle attachment and on low speed add the chocolate mixture slowly. Sift the flour, baking powder, cocoa and spices over the chocolate mixture mix on low speed just until combined-don't over mix. With a silicone spatula, fold in nuts and 1 cup chocolate chips until just mixed-do not over mix or the brownies will be tough. Pour into the 9x9 dish and bake for 35 minutes. Cool completely. Cut, serve and enjoy.

*For cakey brownies omit 1 cup of bittersweet chocolate **Valrhona cocoa powder has the most chocolate flavor and is the least bitter. Sunspire chocolate chips are sweetened without sugar. See

Resources. Available at Whole Foods Market or online.

Ginger Snap Cookies

These are just crunchy enough to qualify as being "snaps", but won't break your teeth! Use for Pumpkin Cheesecake crust or ice cream sandwiches, or eat them as is! Delicious with a cup of Chai Tea.

Yields: 18 cookies

1 ¾ cups oat flour

½ teaspoon baking soda

½ teaspoon baking powder

½ teaspoon sea salt, fine

1 ½ Tablespoons ground ginger

1 teaspoon ground cinnamon

¼ teaspoon whole nutmeg, grated

¼ teaspoon ground cloves

1/3 cup grapeseed oil

½ cup real maple syrup, grade B dark

2 Tablespoons unsulfured molasses

1 teaspoon real vanilla extract

Preheat oven to 350 degrees. Sift all dry ingredients into the bowl of an electric stand mixer. Add wet ingredients and mix with a paddle attachment just until combined. Scrape down bowl and mix briefly. With a 1 Tablespoon size ice cream scooper, scoop dough onto a baking sheet evenly spacing 9 onto each pan. Bake one pan at a time on the middle rack of the oven for 12-14 minutes or until golden brown on the bottom, but not burned. They will still feel soft in the middle, but will get crispy when cool. Remove from pan onto a wire cooling rack. Eat warm while a little soft or wait a few minutes if you like them crispy! Dunk in a cold glass of Almond Milk or a hot cup of Chai Tea! Make ice cream sandwiches with vanilla ice "cream" (see index).

Gingerbread Molasses Cake

This cake is so moist that it doesn't even need any frosting, but a scoop of vanilla "ice cream" is delicious! Great with a cup of tea! The smell will transport you to your Grandmother's house! Nancy, this one is dedicated to you!

1 cup pure maple syrup, Grade B dark

½ cup unsulfured molasses

½ cup vegan Earth Balance or vegetable shortening, melted and cooled

2 lg. organic eggs, beaten

1 teaspoon real vanilla extract

1 cup boiling bottled or filtered water

2 cups oat flour

2 teaspoon baking soda

½ teaspoon sea salt, fine

1 teaspoon ground cinnamon

½ teaspoon ground cloves

½ teaspoon ground ginger

Preheat oven to 350 degrees. Measure out all wet ingredients, except for the boiling water, into a mixing bowl. Sift all dry ingredients into the wet ingredients. Mix by hand with a silicone spatula. Add boiling water and stir just until mixed. Batter will be very thin. Pour into a greased and floured 9 ½ x 13 inch glass baking dish. Bake immediately for about 30 minutes. Check it at 25 minutes and test with a toothpick. When the toothpick comes out clean it is done. Cool on a wire rack for at least 15 minutes. Serve warm or cold. Delicious with a scoop of vanilla "ice cream" (see index)!

Key Lime Curd

A silky, rich and tart curd that will transport you to the Florida Keys!

Yields: 2 cups

½ cup key lime juice

1 ½ cups sucanat, honey or 1 cup agave nectar

4 lg. organic eggs, beaten

1 stick vegan Earth Balance, cold/cubed

1 Tablespoon key lime zest

Wash limes with vegetable wash and rinse well. Zest the key limes with a microplane grater or zester, set aside. In saucepot, heat juice to simmer over low heat. Whisk eggs and sweetener together in a bowl. Remove pot from heat and quickly whisk in all of egg/sweetener mixture. Whisk continuously over low heat until thickened, about 3 minutes and remove from heat. Whisk in one cube of Earth Balance at a time until melted. Pour through a fine strainer into a bowl. Stir zest into curd. Ladle or spoon into heatproof glass bowl or ceramic containers, cover and refrigerate until set.

Enjoy over scones or use for cake or Key Lime Pie/ Tart filling. Spoon over cheesecake or serve with fresh fruit and berries.

Key Lime Meringue Tart

This tart has a sour filling, sweet, fluffy topping and a crispy crust! It's delicious any time of year- refreshing in the summer and great in the winter when limes are in season!

Yields: 1-10 inch tart, serves 8-10

1 recipe sweet tart dough, chilled (see index)

1 recipe key lime curd, room temperature* (see index)

1 recipe meringue (see index)

Roll out tart dough and place in tart pan, and press excess dough off the edges of the pan. Refrigerate for 30 minutes to prevent shrinking. Preheat oven to 350 degrees. Place a piece of parchment over dough and pour dry beans, uncooked rice or pie weights on top of parchment. Bake for 20 minutes on the middle rack. Remove from oven and take out the dried beans and parchment. Continue to bake for approximately 10 more minutes or until golden brown. Cool completely on a rack at room temperature. Fill crust with key lime curd and refrigerate for 2 hours. Make meringue and pipe or spoon over key lime curd. Cut and serve immediately or refrigerate for 1-8 hours. If you wish, you can brown the meringue with a kitchen torch or under a broiler for 2 minutes until golden brown. Enjoy!

*If you make the curd the day you assemble the tart, cool to room temperature and pour it into the shell, and it will set evenly and glossy when refrigerated. If you are short on time, make the curd ahead of time and smooth with an offset spatula. Don't worry most of it will be covered with meringue anyway.

To save time, make the tart dough 1 day to 1 week ahead and keep refrigerated.

Lavender Honey "Ice Cream"

This will transport you to Provence, France where it is served often! While teaching culinary school, my students thought this was going to be terrible, but after tasting it- they begged me to make it every week!

Yields: 1 quart

Special Equipment: Ice cream maker or Kitchen Aid frozen ice cream bowl attachment with paddle, glass pitcher.

2 cups regular coconut milk*

1 ½ cups light coconut milk, chilled

½ cup lavender honey or agave nectar and 2 Tablespoons organic lavender blossoms

6 lg. organic egg yolks

In a saucepan, heat 1 2/3 cup regular coconut milk, ½ cup agave nectar and lavender blossoms or honey over medium-high heat until it simmers (170 degrees). Set aside and let steep for one hour. Strain out the lavender blossoms and pour mixture back into the saucepan, heat to 170 degrees.

In an electric mixer, with whisk attachment, beat egg yolks on medium-high or speed 6 about 5 minutes until pale and light and a thick ribbon runs off the whisk when lifted. Reduce to low speed and slowly drizzle in 1 cup of hot coconut milk/honey or agave.

Pour egg/coconut milk mixture back into saucepan of the remaining coconut milk. Whisk constantly over medium-high heat until it is thick and at 180 degrees. Dip a spoon into mixture and wipe a clean line across the middle of the spoon. If the line stays clean and the mixture does not run down into the line, it's done, otherwise continue to cook a little longer and test every minute. If you overcook it, it will curdle. Add remaining chilled light coconut milk. Pour into a glass pitcher, cover mixture and refrigerate 6 hours or until 38 degrees. Be sure you have a thermometer in your refrigerator and keep it between 34-38 degrees-over 40 degrees is optimal temperature for bacterial growth!

Follow the manufacturer's ice cream machine instructions to churn. When finished churning, pour into plastic containers and freeze for 8 hours or overnight for premium ice cream texture, or eat a little of it now, which will be soft serve consistency. Scoop and enjoy!

*Note: you can use all light coconut milk, but the texture will not be as creamy.

Lemon Curd

A tart-sweet silky curd that tastes like a lemon drop candy!

Yields: 4 cups

2 cups freshly squeezed lemon juice

2 cups sucanat or honey or 1 ½ cups agave nectar

12 organic lg. eggs, beaten

3 sticks vegan Earth Balance, cold/cubed or 1 cup lemon olive oil

Wash lemons with vegetable wash and rise well. Zest lemons with microplane fine grater, set aside. Juice lemons and remove seeds, set aside. In a mixing bowl, whisk eggs and sweetener. In saucepot, heat juice to simmer over low heat. Remove pot from heat and quickly pour in all of egg/sweetener mixture while whisking vigorously. Whisk continuously over low heat until thickened, about 3-5 minutes. Whisk in one pat of vegan Earth Balance at a time until melted or slowly pour in oil while whisking. Pour through a fine strainer into a bowl. Stir in zest. Ladle or spoon into heatproof glass or ceramic containers, cover and refrigerate until set.

Variations: you can substitute lemon juice for fresh grapefruit juice. Also substitute with the same citrus zest and citrus olive oil.

This makes a great filling for Lemon Meringue Pie/ Tart (see index)! Enjoy over scones or use for cake or tart filling. Serve with fresh fruit and berries.

Lemon Meringue Tart

This tart has a sour filling, sweet, fluffy topping and a crispy crust! It's delicious any time of year- refreshing in the summer and great in the winter when lemons are in season!

Yields: 1-10 inch tart, serves 8-10

1 recipe sweet tart dough, chilled (see index)

1 recipe lemon curd, room temperature* (see index)

1 recipe meringue (see index)

Roll out tart dough and place in tart pan and press excess dough off the edges. Refrigerate for 30 minutes to prevent shrinking. Preheat oven to 350 degrees. Place a piece of parchment over dough and pour dry beans, uncooked rice or pie weights on top of parchment. Bake for 20 minutes on the middle rack. Remove from oven and take out the dried beans and parchment. Continue to bake for approximately 10 more minutes or until golden brown. Cool completely on a rack at room temperature. Fill crust with lemon curd and refrigerate for 2 hours. Make meringue and pipe or spoon over lemon curd. Cut and serve immediately or refrigerate for 1-8 hours. If you wish, you can brown the meringue with a kitchen torch or under a broiler for 2 minutes until golden brown. Enjoy!

*If you make the curd the day you assemble the tart, cool to room temperature and pour it into the shell, and it will set evenly and glossy when refrigerated. If you are short on time, make the curd ahead of time and smooth with an offset spatula. Don't worry most of it will be covered with meringue anyway.

To save time, make the tart dough 1 day to 1 week ahead and keep refrigerated.

Linzer Raspberry Tart

I first enjoyed this dessert in little café while working in Switzerland! The combination of a nutty crust and the raspberry jam is delightful, especially with a hot cup of coffee or tea. I keep this dough in the freezer and a jar of fruit spread in my pantry at all times for unexpected guests or a quick dessert when I am short on time and or money!

Yields: 1 (10 inch) tart or 4 (4 inch) tarts

1 ½ cups oat flour

½ cup ground almonds or almond meal

1 ½ sticks (12 Tablespoons) vegan Earth Balance or vegetable shortening cubed, chilled

3 Tablespoons agave nectar or 4 Tablespoons sucanat or date sugar

2 organic egg yolks

2 Tablespoons iced water

1 teaspoon ground cinnamon

½ cup raspberry fruit spread (no sugar added)

Place all ingredients except raspberry fruit spread, into a food processor, fitted with s blade, and pulse just until it comes together and forms a ball. Scrape all dough onto a large piece of plastic wrap and form into a ball, and flatten to 1 inch thick. Refrigerate for at least 1 hour. It can be frozen for later use, and defrosted in the refrigerator overnight. Remove from refrigerator, cut in half and place one half back in the refrigerator for the lattice later. Roll the other half out to ¼ inch thick between two pieces of plastic wrap or on a well floured board. Place in tart pan and press it into the sides all the way to the top. Cover and refrigerate for 30 minutes. Take out the tart pan and unrolled dough. Roll the remaining dough out to ¼ inch thick. Using a pastry cutter, straight or fluted, cut ½ inch strips across the dough. Pour ½ cup of fruit spread into the tart shell and spread evenly with a spoon or offset spatula. Place half the strips of dough across the tart, evenly spaced, like a white picket fence with a ½ inch space between each strip. Place the remaining strips diagonally across the top of the other strips. Be sure to press the ends of the strips into the edge of the pan. Chill the tart in the refrigerator 30 minutes. Preheat oven to 350 degrees and bake approximately 25 minutes or until it is golden brown. Cool tart completely on a wire rack. Slice into wedges like a pie and enjoy. Delicious with vanilla ice "cream" (see index).

Madeline Cookies

These cookies are like little seashell cakes. They are wonderful with a cup of tea. I like to give them as gift for my guests to take home along with the recipe. This recipe was inspired by a very talented Master French Chef I worked for while studying in culinary school.

Yields: 12 large or 24 small Madelines

1 ¼ cups almond meal or ground pistachios

1 ¾ cups oat flour

1 cup agave nectar

5 organic egg whites, room temperature

½ cup lemon olive oil or 1 ½ sticks vegan earth balance, melted and cooled

1 Tablespoon honey (clover or orange)

1 teaspoon real vanilla extract

zest of one lemon

Preheat oven to 350 degrees. Grease Madeline pan with vegan earth balance being sure to get all the grooves coated. Dust pan with oat flour and tap out extra over the kitchen sink or trash can-do not skip this step or they will stick, I promise! Sift the flour into a mixing bowl and add almond or pistachio meal. Stir agave nectar into dry mixture to combine. Add one egg white at a time stirring until it is incorporated completely. Stir in olive oil or vegan Earth Balance, honey, vanilla and zest. Fill each shell completely. Bake for approximately 12 minutes or until golden brown. Cool on a wire rack until you can touch the pan. Gently push the Madelines from the bottom and it should slip out. Continue to cool completely on a wire rack. Delicious with a cup of tea or coffee.

Mango Crisp

This is my favorite fruit dessert to eat and share. This transports me to a tropical beach vacation! Serve with vanilla ice "cream" (see index).

Yields: 1 (9x12) pan or 2 quart round soufflé dish- serves 6-10 people

Filling:

3 pounds fresh or frozen mango, 1/2 inch cubes

1/3 cup agave nectar

1 teaspoon real vanilla extract

 zest and juice of 1 lemon

1 teaspoon tapioca starch or 2 Tablespoons oat or barley flour

Topping:

1 cup oat or barley flour, sifted

½ cup date sugar or maple sugar or sucanat

1 stick vegan Earth Balance, cold or frozen and diced

zest of one lemon

1 teaspoon vanilla powder, optional

¼ teaspoon freshly grated nutmeg

¼ teaspoon ground cinnamon

½ cup chopped nuts (walnuts, pecans, almonds, macadamia)

½ cup old fashioned rolled oats (not quick cooking)

Preheat oven to 350 degrees. Wash lemons and fruit with vegetable wash. Do you know how many people have handled that fruit? Trust me, you don't want to know...just wash it and rinse well with cold water! Slice fruit and put in a large bowl and add the rest of the filling ingredients to the fruit, stir well. Pour into a 9x12 glass baking dish or a 2 quart round soufflé dish or something equivalent-it can be a different shape, but the same size. Set fruit aside.

For the topping, place all ingredients into a food processor with the s blade, and pulse until it is crumbly and the size of cherries. Pour evenly over fruit and bake for approximately 30 minutes or until the topping is golden brown and fruit is bubbling. This must be cooled for 1 hour.

Meringue

This fluffy topping can be used over tarts and pies. A great substitute for whipped cream with a lot less calories too! Great on top of a lemon or key lime tart (see index).

Yields: enough for 1 10 inch tart or pie

4 lg. organic egg whites or Eggology whites, at room temperature*

¼ cup honey or agave nectar

Wash and dry the bowl and whisk attachment of an electric stand mixer to be sure it is very clean and completely dry so egg whites will whip well. Pour the honey or agave into a saucepot and insert a candy thermometer that the end is just above the bottom of the pot. Place the pot over medium heat and wait for it to start bubbling around the edges. When the honey reaches 245 degrees begin to whip the egg whites in an electric mixer on medium high speed until a soft peak. A soft peak is when the whites are foamy and the tip of the meringue on top of the whip falls over slightly when turned upside down. When honey is at 250 degrees, remove from heat and with the electric mixer on medium low speed slowly pour the honey in a small stream next to the side of the bowl, being careful not to pour it over the whisk itself. Whip the meringue on medium speed until the outside of the bowl is warm, but not hot-approximately 5-8 minutes. It should be glossy and fluffy and stand up without falling.

Spoon or pipe the meringue, with a large star tip, in a piping bag over a tart or pie. This will keep in the refrigerator for 1-2 days and will begin to weep and separate after that. Keep refrigerated. To brown meringue a torch works best, or place under broiler for 2 minutes or less.

Note: Do NOT try to make this on a rainy day or when there is high humidity. It will not work and the whites will separate. Trust me on this one. Just before my photo shoot for this book it was raining for 3 days! Just one example of some of the challenges of writing a cookbook!

I like this method of cooking the honey or agave because it holds up better than uncooked sugar and it kills the bacteria in the egg whites which is much safer.

*Place eggs or container into a bowl of very warm to hot water until they are not cold to the touch. This will only take a few minutes.

Mocha "Ice Cream"

This is for people who just can't choose between chocolate and coffee because they love them both! A luscious combination of espresso coffee and chocolate in a creamy frozen state...what's not to love about that?

Yields: 1 quart

Special Equipment: Ice cream maker or Kitchen Aid frozen ice cream bowl attachment with paddle, glass pitcher.

2 cups regular coconut milk*

1 ½ cups light coconut milk, chilled

6 Tablespoons instant espresso*

1/3 cup Valrhona cocoa powder

6 oz. organic dark chocolate 70%+, finely chopped**

½ cup agave nectar or clover honey

6 lg. organic egg yolks

1 teaspoon real vanilla extract

In a saucepan, heat 1 2/3 cup regular coconut milk, ½ cup agave nectar or honey over medium-high heat until it simmers (170 degrees). Sift in 1/3 cup cocoa powder, espresso powder and whisk.

In an electric mixer, with whisk attachment, beat egg yolks on medium-high or speed 6 about 5 minutes until pale and light and a thick ribbon runs off the whisk when lifted. Turn down to low speed and slowly drizzle in 1 cup of hot coconut milk/honey.

Pour egg/coconut milk mixture back into saucepan of the remaining coconut milk. Whisking constantly over medium-high heat until it is thick and at 180 degrees. Dip a spoon into mixture and wipe a clean line across the middle of the spoon. If the line stays clean and the mixture does not run down into the line, it's done, otherwise continue to cook a little longer and test every minute. If you overcook it, it will curdle. Remove from heat and pour in chopped chocolate, let sit 1 minute and whisk until smooth. Add remaining chilled light coconut milk, 1 teaspoon real vanilla extract and whisk. Pour into a glass pitcher, cover mixture and refrigerate 6 hours or until it is 38 degrees. Be sure you have a thermometer in your refrigerator and keep it between 34-38 degrees-over 40 degrees is optimal temperature for bacterial growth!

Follow the manufacturer's ice cream machine instructions to churn. When finished churning, pour into plastic containers and freeze for 8 hours or overnight for premium ice cream texture, or eat a little of it now, which will be soft serve consistency. Scoop and enjoy!

*You can use all light coconut milk, but the texture will not be as creamy. You can use instant coffee instead of espresso, but the flavor will not be as pronounced.

**I recommend Valrhona, Dagoba, Callebaut or a combination.

Pastry "Cream"

This flavorful thick rich vanilla cream is the perfect filling for cream puffs and fruit tarts.

Yields: 2 ½ cups

2 lg. organic eggs

2 lg. organic egg yolks

½ cup agave nectar

3 Tablespoons oat flour

2 Tablespoons tapioca starch or cornstarch

2 cups regular coconut milk

½ vanilla bean

1 teaspoon real vanilla extract

1 Tablespoon vegan Earth Balance

In an electric stand mixer, put eggs, yolks, agave, oat flour and tapioca starch and mix on low speed until smooth, occasionally scraping the sides and bottom of the bowl. Cut the vanilla bean in half lengthwise and scrape the seeds out with the back of a knife. Put vanilla bean and seeds into the coconut milk. Pour the coconut milk into a 2 quart sauce pot bring to a boil over high heat then, carefully remove vanilla bean pod. With electric mixer on medium speed pour half the hot coconut milk into the egg mixture. Pour the egg mixture into the sauce pot of remaining coconut milk and whisking constantly over medium heat for approximately 2 minutes or until it is very thick. Whisk in the vegan Earth Balance and vanilla extract until well combined. Strain it through a fine mesh sieve into a glass or ceramic bowl and cover with plastic wrap directly over the top of the pastry cream to prevent a skin from forming. Cool to room temperature for approximately 30 minutes then, refrigerate until cold, about 2 hours or more. Use to fill cream puffs (see index), pies, tarts or cake filling.

Peach Pie

There is nothing like a warm piece of peach pie with a scoop of vanilla ice "cream" on top! It's simply mouth watering!

Yields: 1 peach pie

1 recipe piecrust (see index)

12 organic peaches or nectarines cored and sliced ½-1 inch thick

½ cup agave nectar or ¾ cup sucanat

zest and juice of 1 lemon

1 ½ teaspoons ground cinnamon

¼ grated whole nutmeg

2 Tablespoons vegan Earth Balance

For top of crust: optional

1 large egg, beaten

2 tablespoons sucanat or maple sugar or date sugar

Roll out one pie crust to ¼ inch thick*. Put it into pie dish and cut the crust along the edge of the pie dish. In a large bowl mix all ingredients except egg and 2 tbsp sucanat. Pour filling into pie shell. Dot with vegan Earth Balance. Roll out the other pie crust and cut a hole in center of remaining crust with a piping tip or biscuit cutter about 1" in diameter, or cut several vents across top of the pie. Put crust over peach filling. Crimp edges with your clean thumb and fingers or the ends of a fork to seal the two crusts. Put pie in freezer for ½-1 hour. Ten minutes before baking, preheat oven to 375 degrees. Immediately before baking, brush pie with egg and sprinkle with sucanat or maple/date sugar. Place pie on a baking sheet in case it bubbles over. Bake pie for 1 hour on the second from the bottom shelf of the oven. Bake until the crust is golden brown and filling is bubbling. Cool on rack for at least one hour. Serve with vanilla ice "cream" (see index).

*Roll the crust on a well floured board or between two pieces of plastic wrap.

Pecan Pie

A true Southern tradition and favorite! A flaky crust holds a dark flavorful maple filling topped with crunchy pecans! Dad, this one is for you!

Yields: 2 pies

1 recipe pie crust (see index)

6 lg. organic eggs

1 1/3 cups sucanat or 1 cup agave nectar

1/16 teaspoon sea salt

2 cups real maple syrup, Grade B dark*

2/3 cup vegan Earth Balance, melted and cooled

2 cups pecans halves, shelled

Preheat oven to 350 degrees

Put pie crusts into two pie dishes, crimp edges.

Whisk all ingredients, except pecans, in a large bowl. Gently stir pecans into the filling. Pour equal amounts of filling into pie shells. Bake for 50 minutes. Insert a knife halfway between the edge of the pie and the center of the pie, when it comes out clean, it is done. Cool on wire rack at least a few hours or overnight. You can put them into the refrigerator if you are in a hurry. Slice and enjoy alone or a la mode with vanilla ice "cream" (see index).

*Dark Grade B Maple Syrup has a deeper more pronounced flavor. I do not use corn syrup ever because it blocks the body's metabolism. Studies have also shown that there is a direct correlation with the increased incidence of diabetes and high fructose corn syrup being added into our food! Read labels because it is in many packaged foods.

Pie Crust

This delicate, flakey pie crust can be made by hand, or in a food processor which is much faster. I learned how to make this from my Aunt. Her desserts are perfection and the whole family always looks forward to enjoying them at gatherings and holidays!

Yields: 2 single crusts

3 cups oat flour

½ teaspoon sea salt, fine

2 sticks vegan Earth Balance or 1 cup vegetable shortening, frozen and diced

½ cup iced water (bottled or filtered)

Put bowl and pastry cutter into the freezer while measuring out ingredients. Try to handle dough as little as possible. You want to keep the pieces of Earth Balance or shortening cold, which will make the crust flakey rather than tough. Sift flour and salt into a large glass or metal mixing bowl or food processor. Add ½ cup shortening or 1 stick Earth Balance and cut into the flour with a pastry cutter, or pulse with food processor, until it is the size and texture of cornmeal. Add remaining ½ cup shortening or stick Earth Balance and cut into the flour with cutter, or pulse with food processor, until it is the size of small green peas. Slowly drizzle 1 Tablespoon of water at a time and blend just until dough forms a ball or comes together so it doesn't break apart. Take a tablespoon of dough, roll it out and if it cracks or falls apart, you need more water. If the dough is sticky, you added too much water-add 1-2 Tablespoons of flour if it is too sticky. The humidity in the air will determine how much water you will need. Cut dough in half and wrap in plastic and refrigerate or put into a freezer zip bag and freeze until ready to use. Thaw in refrigerator for 8 hours.

When ready to make the pie:

Between two pieces of plastic wrap or on a well floured board, roll out the dough -when rolling dough, roll once with even pressure and turn a quarter turn and continue rolling and turning until it is ¼ inch thick. If it sticks, add more flour to board. Only roll out one time or it will become tough instead of flakey. Brush off any excess flour with a dry pastry or basting brush. If using plastic remove the top piece of plastic and lift up the bottom piece of plastic holding the dough and flip it over into a pie pan and peel off the plastic. If using a floured board, gently roll the dough around the rolling pin, start at the edge of the pie pan, and unroll it over the pie pan. If it sticks to the board, slide a long flat spatula under it. Roll out remaining half of dough after you have filled the pie and are ready to bake it. Dough can be frozen up to 6 months if double wrapped in plastic and then put into a zip freezer bag. It will keep in the refrigerator for a few days.

Pina Colada Cake

My Mom came up with this brilliant idea when I was a child and it was a huge hit with everyone. This is my version that was inspired by my Mom. Mom, this one is dedicated to you!

Yields: 1 (9x13) cake or two 8 inch round cakes

3 ½ cups oat flour

2 teaspoons baking soda

2 teaspoons baking powder

1 teaspoon sea salt, fine

1 cup shredded unsweetened coconut, optional

¼ cup grapeseed oil

2/3 cup agave nectar

1 ½ cups coconut milk (regular or light)

½ cup unsweetened pineapple juice

2 teaspoons apple cider vinegar

1 teaspoon real vanilla extract or 1 vanilla bean

zest of 1 washed orange

1 Tablespoon dark or white rum or 1 teaspoon rum extract, optional

1 recipe Buttercream (see index)

2 cups toasted coconut for topping*

Preheat oven to 350 degrees. Oil pan with vegan Earth Balance or grapeseed oil, then dust with oat flour and tap out any excess. Sift all dry ingredients, except coconut, orange zest and buttercream, into the bowl of an electric stand mixer. Add 1 cup coconut and orange zest. Measure out all liquid ingredients and add to dry ingredients. If using vanilla bean, cut in half lengthwise and scrape out seeds with the back of a knife. Whisk the vanilla bean into the wet ingredients. Place paddle attachment onto mixer and mix on low speed just until incorporated. Stop mixer and scrape down sides and bottom of the bowl, mix briefly until smooth. Pour batter into cake pan and bake on the middle rack of oven for 40 minutes. Insert a toothpick in the middle of the cake and it is done when it comes out clean. If it does not come out clean continue baking approximately 5 more minutes and continue to check until it is done. Cool on a wire rack until completely cool. Remove from round pans. You can keep it in the 9x13 pan. Frost with "buttercream" and top with toasted coconut. *Put coconut on a baking sheet and broil until golden brown, be careful it burns fast. You can freeze a well wrapped, unfrosted cake for up to 1 month in a plastic freezer zip bag.

Pina Colada Cupcakes

My Mom came up with this brilliant idea when I was a child and it was a huge hit with everyone. This is my version that was inspired by my Mom. These cupcakes are wrapped in their own package!

Yields: 24 cupcakes, regular size

3 ½ cups oat flour

2 teaspoons baking soda

2 teaspoons baking powder

1 teaspoon sea salt, fine

1 cup shredded unsweetened coconut, optional

¼ cup grapeseed oil

2/3 cup agave nectar

1 ½ cups coconut milk (regular or light)

½ cup pineapple juice

2 teaspoons apple cider vinegar

1 teaspoon real vanilla extract or 1 vanilla beans

zest of 1 washed orange

1 Tablespoon dark or white rum or 1 teaspoon rum extract, optional

1 recipe Buttercream Frosting (see index) + 2 cups toasted shredded coconut for topping*

Preheat oven to 350 degrees. Oil cupcake pan with vegan Earth Balance or grapeseed oil or insert paper liners into cups. Sift all dry ingredients, except coconut, orange zest and buttercream, into the bowl of an electric stand mixer. Add coconut and orange zest. Measure out all liquid ingredients and add to dry ingredients. If using vanilla beans, cut in half lengthwise and scrape out seeds with the back of a knife. Whisk the vanilla bean into the wet ingredients. Place paddle attachment onto mixer and mix on low speed just until incorporated. Stop mixer and scrape down sides and bottom of the bowl, mix briefly until smooth. Pour batter ¾ of the way up the cups in the cupcake pan and bake on top of a baking sheet on the middle rack of oven for 20 minutes. Insert a toothpick in the middle of the cupcake and it is done when it comes out clean. If it does not come out clean continue baking approximately 5 more minutes and check until they are done. Cool completely on a wire rack. Frost with "buttercream" and sprinkle with toasted coconut. *Put coconut on a baking sheet and broil until golden brown, be careful it burns fast.

Pumpkin Cheesecake

A light and creamy filling with the flavor of Pumpkin Pie on top of a spicy Ginger Snap crust! This is the most popular recipe from the cookbook with all my friends! A true crowd pleaser even for those who are not big fans of dessert! Ernesto and Toti, this one is especially for you!

Yields: 1 cheesecake (10 inches)

1 ½ cups ginger snap cookie crumbs (see index)

¾ cup pecans or walnuts, chopped or ¾ cup cookie crumbs

3 Tablespoons sucanat or maple sugar or date sugar

½ stick vegan Earth Balance or vegetable margarine, melted and cooled

24 oz. soy cream cheese*

1 cup agave nectar

3 lg. organic eggs

1/8 cup regular coconut milk

15 oz. organic pumpkin puree (not pie filling)

1 teaspoon real vanilla extract

1 Tablespoon Cognac or Brandy, optional but highly recommended

½ teaspoon sea salt, fine

1 Tablespoon ground cinnamon

1 teaspoon whole nutmeg, freshly grated

2 teaspoons ground ginger

Preheat oven to 350 degrees. Melt and cool Earth Balance to room temperature. In food processor, with the s blade, process pecans until finely chopped, put in a bowl and set aside. Process cookie crumbs until they are a fine crumb, pour into nuts. Add sucanat and melted Earth Balance to nut mixture and stir until combined. Pour into springform pan and press it down on the bottom and half way up the sides. Set aside. In an electric stand mixer, with the paddle attachment, mix soy cream cheese and agave until smooth and creamy. Scrape down the sides and bottom of bowl and continue to mix. Add eggs, one at a time and mix. Add all the rest of the ingredients and mix until smooth. Gently pour into the springform pan. Tap on counter to release air bubbles. Put on a baking sheet and bake on the middle rack of the oven for 50 minutes. Remove from oven and cool on a wire rack to room temperature. Chill overnight or at least 4 hours in the refrigerator. Delicious accompanied by a warm cup of tea or coffee. Great to bring to a party-you will be a hero!

*Tofutti brand was used when testing this recipe.

Pumpkin "Ice Cream"

This ice cream is great in the fall or an alternative to pumpkin pie!

Yields: 1 quart

Special Equipment: Ice cream maker or Kitchen Aid frozen ice cream bowl attachment with paddle, glass pitcher.

2 cups regular coconut milk*

1 ½ cups light coconut milk, chilled

¾-1 cup clover honey or agave nectar

1 ½ cups organic pumpkin puree (solid pack)*

½ teaspoon ground cinnamon

½ teaspoon ground ginger

¼ teaspoon whole nutmeg, grated

1/8 teaspoon ground cloves

6 lg. organic egg yolks

1 teaspoon real vanilla extract

In a saucepan, heat 1 2/3 cup regular coconut milk, ¾ cup agave nectar or honey over medium-high heat until it simmers (170 degrees). In an electric mixer, with whisk attachment, beat egg yolks on medium-high or speed 6 about 5 minutes until pale and light and a thick ribbon runs off the whisk when lifted. Reduce to low speed 2 and slowly drizzle in 1 cup of hot coconut milk/honey. Pour egg/coconut milk mixture back into saucepan of the remaining coconut milk. Add all spices. Whisk constantly over medium-high heat until it is thick and at 180 degrees. Dip a spoon into mixture and wipe a clean line across the middle of the spoon. If the line stays clean and the mixture does not run down into the line, it's done, otherwise continue to cook a little longer and test every minute. If you overcook it, it will curdle. Whisk in pumpkin puree. Add remaining chilled light coconut milk and vanilla extract and whisk until combined. Taste for sweetness and whisk in remaining ¼ cup of honey or agave if needed. Pour into a glass pitcher and cover mixture and refrigerate 6 hours or until 38 degrees. Be sure you have a thermometer in your refrigerator and keep it between 34-38 degrees-over 40 degrees is optimal temperature for bacterial growth!

Follow the manufacturer's ice cream machine instructions to churn. When finished churning, pour into plastic containers and freeze for 8 hours or overnight for premium ice cream texture, or eat a little of it now, which will be soft serve consistency. Scoop and enjoy!

*Note: you can use all light coconut milk, but the texture will not be as creamy.

*Do not substitute pumpkin pie filling

Pumpkin Pie

This pie is light and silky with all the holiday spices and flavor on a flaky crust!

Yields: 1 Pie

1 15oz can organic pumpkin*

2 Lg. organic eggs, beaten

1 cup unsweetened vanilla almond milk**

½ cup real maple syrup or 1/3 cup dark agave nectar***

1 teaspoon ground cinnamon

½ teaspoon grated whole nutmeg

¼ teaspoon ground ginger

1/8 teaspoon ground cloves

1 teaspoon sea salt, fine

1 single pie crust (see index)

In an electric mixer, fitted with the paddle attachment, blend all ingredients except pie crust together on low speed, mixing well. You can do this by hand with a whisk or hand held mixer on low. Do not over beat. Pour into pie shell. Bake on second from bottom shelf at 425 degrees for 15 minutes, and then reduce temperature to 350 degrees and bake for an additional 45 minutes. Cool on a wire rack.

Cover and refrigerate. A holiday favorite! Fabulous a la mode with vanilla ice cream (see index)! Also delicious for breakfast with a cup of hot tea or coffee-hey, it's a vegetable!

*Do not use Pumpkin Pie Filling

**You can use rice or soy milk

***Maple syrup has the most flavor, but agave has a lower glycemic index and many diabetics can tolerate agave-check with your physician first.

Rhubarb Crisp

I wait all year for Rhubarb to arrive at my local Farmer's Market in the springtime! If you've never tried rhubarb, try this recipe-you'll love it! Serve with vanilla or strawberry ice "cream".

Yields: 1 (9x12) pan or 2 quart round soufflé dish-serves 6-10 people

Filling:

3 pounds of fresh or frozen rhubarb, 1 inch slices

3/4 cup agave nectar

1 teaspoon real vanilla extract

 zest and juice of 1 lemon

1 teaspoon tapioca starch or 2 Tablespoons oat or barley flour

Topping:

1 cup oat or barley flour, sifted

½ cup sucanat or date sugar or maple sugar

1 stick vegan Earth Balance, cold or frozen and diced

zest of one lemon

1 teaspoon vanilla powder, optional

¼ teaspoon freshly grated whole nutmeg

¼ teaspoon ground cinnamon

½ cup chopped nuts (walnuts, pecans, almonds)

½ cup old fashioned rolled oats (not quick cooking)

Preheat oven to 350 degrees. Wash lemons and fruit with vegetable wash. Do you know how many people have handled that fruit? Trust me, you don't want to know...just wash it and rinse well with cold water! Slice fruit and put in a large bowl and add the rest of the filling ingredients to the fruit, stir well. Pour into a 9x12 glass baking dish or a 2 quart round soufflé dish or something equivalent-it can be a different shape, but the same size. Set fruit aside.

For the topping, place all ingredients into a food processor with the s blade, and pulse until it is crumbly and the size of cherries. You can also use a bowl and a pastry cutter instead of a food processor. Pour evenly over fruit and bake for approximately 30 minutes or until the topping is golden brown and fruit is bubbling. This must be cooled for 1 hour to set. Serve with ice "cream" (see index). Rhubarb leaves have a high level of oxalic acid which is poisonous and must not be eaten. Just eat the stalks which are best cooked.

Rocky Road "Ice Cream"

As if dark chocolate ice cream is not satisfying enough, just add marshmallows and almonds for a little more fun and crunch! Kids love this!

Yields: 1 quart

Special Equipment: Ice cream maker or Kitchen Aid frozen ice cream bowl attachment with paddle, glass pitcher.

2 cups regular coconut milk*

1 ½ cups light coconut milk, chilled

1/3 cup Valrhona cocoa powder

6 oz. dark chocolate (70%+), finely chopped**

½ cup agave nectar or clover honey

6 lg. organic egg yolks

1 tsp. real vanilla extract

½ cup mini kosher marshmallow or large kosher marshmallows cut into 4-6 pieces each

½ cup chopped almonds, toasted

In a saucepan, heat 1 2/3 cup regular coconut milk, ½ cup agave nectar or honey over medium-high heat until it simmers (170 degrees). Sift in 1/3 cup cocoa powder and whisk.

In an electric mixer, with whisk attachment, beat egg

yolks on medium-high or speed 6 about 5 minutes until pale and light and a thick ribbon runs off the whisk when lifted. Reduce to low speed and slowly drizzle in 1 cup of hot coconut milk/honey.

Pour egg/coconut milk mixture back into saucepan of the remaining coconut milk. Whisk constantly over medium-high heat until it is thick and at 180 degrees. Dip a spoon into mixture and wipe a clean line across the middle of the spoon. If the line stays clean and the mixture does not run down into the line, it's done, otherwise continue to cook a little longer and test every minute. If you overcook it, it will curdle. Remove from heat and pour in chopped chocolate, let sit 1 minute and whisk until smooth. Add remaining chilled light coconut milk, 1 teaspoon real vanilla extract and whisk. Pour into a glass pitcher, cover mixture and refrigerate 6 hours or until 38 degrees. Be sure you have a thermometer in your refrigerator and keep it between 34-38 degrees-over 40 degrees is optimal temperature for bacterial growth!

Follow the manufacturer's ice cream machine instructions to churn. When ice "cream" is soft serve consistency, add marshmallows and almonds. When finished churning, pour into plastic containers and freeze for 8 hours or overnight for premium ice cream texture, or eat a little of it now, which will be soft serve consistency. Scoop and enjoy!

*Note: you can use all light coconut milk, but the texture will not be as creamy.

**I recommend Valrhona, Dagoba, Callebaut or a combination.

Rugelah

Delicate, crumbly little crescents filled with the sweet goodness of raisins and cinnamon!

Yields: 48 cookies

8 ounces soy cream cheese (Tofutti is good), room temperature

2 sticks vegan Earth Balance or 1 cup vegetable shortening, room temperature

¼ cup agave nectar

¼ teaspoon sea salt, fine

2 teaspoons pure vanilla extract

2 cups oat flour

1 ½ teaspoons ground cinnamon

¾ cup raisins, organic and unsulfured if possible

1 cup organic walnut pieces, optional

½ cup apricot fruit spread (fruit juice sweetened)

¾ cup maple sugar or sucanat

Set soy cream cheese and Earth Balance out to come to room temperature for a few hours. In an electric mixer, fitted with paddle attachment on medium low speed, mix the soy cream cheese and Earth Balance until combine and fluffy. On low speed slowly pour the agave nectar into the mixture, and mix until combined. Scrape bowl down to bottom to be sure it is all mixed well. Sift sea salt, ½ teaspoon cinnamon and oat flour into the creamed mixture. Mix on low speed just until combine. Cover the bowl with plastic wrap and refrigerate for 1-2 hours. Do not skip this step.

Filling: Measure out ¾ cup maple sugar or sucanat, 1 teaspoon cinnamon, walnut pieces and raisins into a bowl and mix by hand. Set aside.

Place the dough onto a well floured board and cut into four equal pieces. Keep one to roll out and place the rest back into the bowl and refrigerate. On a well floured board, roll out dough ball into an 8 inch circle by rolling from the center to the edge with even pressure, and turning it one quarter turn. Continue to do this until you have an 8 inch circle. Spread 2 Tablespoons of apricot fruit spread onto the dough with an offset spatula, leaving ¼ inch of an edge clean. Sprinkle the filling evenly over the fruit spread, leaving ¼ inch edge clean. Press the filling down with your clean hands. Cut into quarters and then each quarter into thirds so you have 12 wedges-looks like a pizza. Roll each wedge from large end towards the point. Place onto a parchment lined baking sheet and curve the ends to make a half moon shape. Refrigerate for 1 hour or they will be flat. Continue with the other balls of dough the same way. Preheat oven to 350 degrees. Bake for 18-20 minutes until golden brown. Remove and cool completely on a wire rack. Enjoy these wonderful cookies that are popular on a Jewish table! I love to wrap these up in a decorated plastic bag or tin as a gift.

Variations: Omit raisins and use alternate flavor of fruit spread. Can omit nuts or keep them.

Chocolate: use dairy free chocolate chips or finely chopped bittersweet or dark chocolate

Apricot: use dried apricots, diced finely

Just use your imagination to create your own flavor combinations. Sometimes I choose four different types for one recipe-one flavor for each quarter of dough. Enjoy and have fun!

Shortbread Cookies

A classic favorite without the traditional ingredients, but just as flavorful!

2-3 cups oat flour, sifted*

¼ teaspoon sea salt, fine

2 sticks vegan Earth Balance or 1 cup vegetable shortening, cold and cut into small cubes

½ cup agave nectar

1 teaspoon real vanilla extract

½ teaspoon almond or lemon extract, optional

1 cup ground nuts (almonds, walnuts, pecans), optional-reduce oat flour to 2 cups*

Preheat oven to 350 degrees. In a food processor, fitted with the s blade, put flour, nuts (if using), sea salt and vegan Earth Balance and pulse until the texture is similar to coarse crumbs. Add agave and extracts and process just until it forms a ball. Place on a piece of plastic wrap and roll into a log about 2 inches in diameter. Refrigerate for 4 hours or overnight. This dough can be cut into ¼ inch thick slices or rolled out to ¼ inch thick and cut out with cookie cutters. You can also use a wooden cookie press to imprint a decoration/pattern. Place cookies on a baking sheet and bake on the middle rack for 15-18 minutes or until the bottom is golden brown. Cool completely on a wire rack before eating or storing. They will be soft to the touch when they come out of the oven, but will harden as they cool.

*If using nuts, use 2 cups oat flour, if not using nuts, use 3 cups oat flour.

Strawberry "Ice Cream"

This is best when fresh organic strawberries are in their peak of season, but if you just can't live without it, frozen will work. Spend the extra money on organic strawberries, conventional are heavily sprayed with pesticides.

Yields: 1 quart

Special Equipment: Ice cream maker or Kitchen Aid frozen ice cream bowl attachment with paddle, glass pitcher.

2 cups regular coconut milk*

1 ½ cups light coconut milk, chilled

½ cup agave nectar or clover honey

6 lg. organic egg yolks

2 pints organic fresh strawberries or 4 cups frozen organic strawberries*

1 teaspoon real vanilla extract

1 teaspoon fresh lemon juice

Wash strawberries with vegetable wash, rinse well and remove the hulls/stems.

In a food processor or blender, puree half the fresh strawberries and thinly slice the remaining half. If using frozen strawberries, puree all of them. Set aside.

In a saucepan, heat 1 2/3 cup regular coconut milk, ½ cup agave nectar or honey over medium-high heat until it simmers (170 degrees). If using a vanilla bean, spilt lengthwise and use the back of a knife to scrape out the seeds-put the seeds and pod into the coconut milk to simmer.

In an electric mixer, with whisk attachment, beat egg yolks on medium-high or speed 6 about 5 minutes until pale and light and a thick ribbon runs off the whisk when lifted. Reduce to low speed and slowly drizzle in 1 cup of hot coconut milk/honey.

Pour egg/coconut milk mixture back into saucepan of the remaining coconut milk, remove vanilla bean pod. Whisk constantly over medium-high heat until it is thick and at 180 degrees. Dip a spoon into mixture and wipe a clean line across the middle of the spoon. If the line stays clean and the mixture does not run down into the line, it's done, otherwise continue to cook a little longer and test every minute. If you overcook it, it will curdle. Add remaining chilled light coconut milk, strawberry puree, real vanilla extract, lemon juice and whisk. Stir in the sliced fresh strawberries. Pour into a glass pitcher, cover mixture and refrigerate 6 hours or until 38 degrees. Be sure you have a thermometer in your refrigerator and keep it between 34-38 degrees-over 40 degrees is optimal temperature for bacterial growth!

Follow the manufacturer's ice cream machine

instructions to churn. When finished churning, pour into plastic containers and freeze for 8 hours or overnight for premium ice cream texture, or eat a little of it now, which will be soft serve consistency. Scoop and enjoy!

*Note: you can use all light coconut milk, but the texture will not be as creamy.

Summer Fruit Crisp

I look forward to summer fruits all year long. Who doesn't like warm fruit with a crumbly topping with vanilla ice "cream"?

Yields: 1 (9x12) pan or 2 quart round soufflé dish- serves 6-10 people

Filling:

3 pounds of stone fruit (nectarines, peaches, apricots, plums), 1 inch slices

½ cup agave nectar

1 teaspoon real vanilla extract

 zest and juice of 1 lemon

1 teaspoon tapioca starch or 2 Tablespoons oat or barley flour

Topping:

1 cup oat or barley flour, sifted

½ cup date sugar or maple sugar or sucanat

1 stick vegan Earth Balance, cold or frozen and diced

zest of one lemon

1 teaspoon vanilla powder, optional

¼ teaspoon freshly grated nutmeg

¼ teaspoon ground cinnamon

½ cup chopped nuts (walnuts, pecans, almonds)

½ cup old fashioned rolled oats (not quick cooking)

Preheat oven to 350 degrees. Wash lemons and fruit with vegetable wash. Do you know how many people have handled that fruit? Trust me, you don't want to know...just wash it and rinse well with cold water! Slice fruit and put in a large bowl and add the rest of the filling ingredients to the fruit, stir well. Pour into a 9x12 glass baking dish or a 2 quart round soufflé dish or something equivalent-it can be a different shape, but the same size. Set fruit aside.

For the topping, place all ingredients into a food processor with the s blade, and pulse until it is crumbly and the size of cherries. This can also be done with a pastry cutter in a bowl. Pour evenly over fruit and bake for approximately 30 minutes or until the topping is golden brown and fruit is bubbling. This must be cooled for 1 hour. Prepare ahead of time and freeze then bake later. Increase baking time if frozen to approximately 1 hour.

Sweet Dough for Tarts

This is versatile and tasty sweet dough that may be used for any tarts.

Yields: 2 (10 inch) Tarts or 8 (4 inch) Tarts

3 sticks vegan Earth Balance or 1 ½ cups vegetable shortening

1 cup sucanat or maple sugar or date sugar

1 lg. organic egg

3 cups oat flour

½ teaspoon sea salt, fine

2 teaspoons real vanilla extract

1 teaspoon pure lemon extract*

In an electric stand mixer, fitted with paddle attachment, cream Earth Balance and sucanat until light and fluffy. Occasionally scrape down sides and bottom of bowl for even mixing. Measure flour and salt and set aside. Add egg, vanilla extract and lemon extract on low speed. Gradually add flour on low speed until combined. Stop the mixer and scrape down sides and bottom to be sure it is mixed evenly and mix again. Put dough on a cookie sheet and refrigerate for 1 hour before rolling out or in a plastic freezer zip bag. If you freeze it, thaw it out in the refrigerator overnight. This is great for any fruit tarts, especially lemon meringue! *If you are making a chocolate tart, substitute the lemon extract for orange if you like.

Roll out on a floured board or between two pieces of plastic wrap ¼ inch thick. Take a rolling pin and gently roll the dough around the pin from one side to the other or remove the top layer of plastic wrap and flip over the dough onto the tart pan. Gently roll it over the tart pan evenly and press it in by hand. Chill the tart pan/dough for 30 minutes before baking to prevent shrinking. Bake at 350 degrees until golden brown. See the directions for the tart you are making. Some tarts you can pour the filling in and bake with the raw dough at the same time.

Sweet Potato Pecan Pie

A true southern dessert to die for-wait until you've eaten a piece! This was inspired by one of my favorite chefs, Paul Prudhomme, who is one of the kindest souls I've ever met. When you cannot decide between pumpkin or sweet potato or pecan pie, this is your answer-dilemma solved!

Yields: 1 pie

½ recipe pie crust (see index)

Sweet Potato Filling:

1 cup canned sweet potato

¼ cup agave nectar

1 lg. organic egg, beaten

1 Tablespoon grapeseed oil or orange olive oil

1 teaspoon orange zest

1 Tablespoon real vanilla extract

¼ teaspoon sea salt, fine

¼ teaspoon ground cinnamon

1/8 teaspoon ground allspice

1/8 teaspoon freshly grated whole nutmeg

Pecan Filling:

½ cup agave nectar

¾ cup real maple syrup, dark grade B

2 lg. organic eggs, beaten

1 Tablespoon vegan Earth Balance, melted and cooled

2 teaspoons real vanilla extract

1/16 teaspoon sea salt, fine

1/16 teaspoon ground cinnamon

¾ cup pecan halves or pieces (halves are prettier)

Preheat oven to 325 degrees. Roll out ½ recipe of pie crust and press into an 8 inch glass pie pan crimping the edges with fingers or a fork and refrigerate. In an electric stand mixer, fitted with the paddle attachment, mix all ingredients for sweet potato filling until well combined, about 2 minutes. Set aside. In a separate bowl, combine all pecan pie filling ingredients except pecans. In an electric mixer with the whisk, mix until well combined and opaque approximately 1 minute. Gently stir in pecans by hand. Remove pie crust from refrigerator. Pour sweet potato filling into dough lined pie pan and smooth out evenly with a spoon or offset spatula. Gently pour the pecan filling over the sweet potato filling. Bake pie at 325 for 1 ¾ hours or until a knife inserted in the middle of the pie comes out clean. Pecans will rise to the top when baking, but will settle when cooled. Cool at room temperature for 2 hours and then refrigerate until set, 4-8 more hours. This is best made one day ahead of when you want to serve it. I make this for Thanksgiving every year-even if it is only a few people. Serve a la mode with vanilla ice "cream" (see index). Shh, if there are any leftovers, it's great for breakfast!

Thumbprint Cookies

Delicate nutty cookies filled with fruit spread are a real treat! They make a wonderful gift.

Yields: 24 cookies

1 cup organic almonds or almond meal*

2 cups oat flour

½ teaspoon sea salt, fine

¼ teaspoon ground cinnamon

½ cup maple syrup or agave nectar

½ cup grapeseed oil

1 teaspoon real vanilla extract

1 teaspoon real almond extract

fruit spread (fruit juice sweetened), any flavor

Preheat oven to 350 degrees. Place almonds in food processor and grind to a fine crumb. Sift all dry ingredients into electric stand mixer, add ground almonds and mix. Measure all wet ingredients and pour into dry ingredients. Mix just until combined.

Using a 1 Tablespoon size ice cream scoop, scoop dough onto a cookie sheet. Dip a ½ teaspoon into hot water and make an indentation in the center of each cookie the same size of the ½ teaspoon, dipping it into water each time or it will stick. Place

½ teaspoon fruit spread into each cookie. Bake 12-13 minutes until golden brown on edges. Cool on cookie sheet for 5 minutes and then finish cooling on a wire rack. Do not touch the jam until fully cooled or it will burn you. Enjoy!

*Omit nuts and add 1 cup oat flour

Tiramisu

An Italian pick me up with the taste of espresso, chocolate and brandy between layers of fluffy filling and soft cake! Heaven in a bite! Close your eyes and you will think you are in Italy!

Yields: 1 8x13 pan, serves 12

Meringue (see Index)-double the recipe

8 oz. soy cream cheese (Tofutti), room temperature

½ yellow cake (see Index)

1 ½ teaspoons real vanilla extract

6 shots of espresso (regular or decaf)*

½ cup coffee liqueur (Kahlua)

½ cup brandy or cognac

Cocoa powder (Valrhona) for dusting, approximately ¼ cup

Bake yellow cake and cool completely, good to do this a day ahead. Note: Do not make this on a rainy day or when there is high humidity. Make meringue according to directions set aside. In an electric stand mixer, fitted with the paddle attachment, beat the soy cream cheese until fluffy on medium-high speed. Mix in 1 cup of meringue to lighten the soy cream cheese. Gently fold the meringue into the soy cream cheese and set aside.

Measure the coffee liqueur and brandy, into a 4 cup measuring cup. Stir in vanilla extract and espresso into the brandy mixture, set aside. Cut the yellow cake into 1 inch x 4 inch rectangles, set aside.

Layer:

Place ½ of the cake fingers in the bottom of an 8x13 inch glass dish, and spread them out with approximately 1 inch in between them. Pour half the coffee liquid over the cake and allow it to be absorbed. With an offset spatula or silicone spatula spread ½ the meringue over the cake evenly. Dust the top of the meringue with cocoa powder just to cover. Repeat with the remaining ingredients, ending with a layer of cocoa powder. Cover with plastic wrap and refrigerate for at least 2 hours. This is best served the day it is made, but will keep for a few days if you don't eat it all first! I took this on vacation and must admit that I indulged in eating it 2-3 times a day and was in heaven! No, I did not gain weight because there is very little fat or refined sugar and absolutely no guilt! Bon Appetito!

*I like to use decaf so I don't have the effect of caffeine, but this does defeat the purpose of the intention of a "pick me up".

Vanilla Bean "Ice Cream"

Cold, smooth and creamy with the exotic flavor of vanilla bean! Add a scoop to any dessert or enjoy alone. Who doesn't love a Hot Fudge Sundae? Pour Chocolate Ganache over a scoop of Ice Cream and enjoy! Want a Banana Split? Add a fresh banana, Raspberry Sauce and Chocolate Ganache (see index for all recipes)! Yummy!

Yields: 1 quart

Special Equipment: Ice cream maker or Kitchen Aid frozen ice cream bowl attachment with paddle, glass pitcher.

2 cups regular coconut milk*

1 ½ cups light coconut milk, chilled

½ cup agave nectar or clover honey

6 lg. organic egg yolks

1 Tablespoon real vanilla extract or 2 vanilla beans

In a saucepan, heat 1 2/3 cup regular coconut milk, ½ cup agave nectar or honey over medium-high heat until it simmers (170 degrees). If using a vanilla bean, spilt lengthwise and use the back of a knife to scrape out the seeds-put the seeds and pod into the coconut milk to simmer. After it comes to a simmer, remove vanilla bean pods and set aside.

In an electric stand mixer, with whisk attachment,

beat egg yolks on medium-high or speed 6 about 5 minutes until pale and light and a thick ribbon runs off the whisk when lifted. Reduce to low speed and slowly drizzle in 1 cup of hot coconut milk/honey.

Pour egg/coconut milk mixture back into saucepan of the remaining coconut milk, remove vanilla bean pod. Whisk constantly over medium-high heat until it is thick and at 180 degrees. Dip a spoon into mixture and wipe a clean line across the middle of the spoon. If the line stays clean and the mixture does not run down into the line, it's done, otherwise continue to cook a little longer and test every minute. If you overcook it, it will curdle. Add remaining chilled light coconut milk, 1 tablespoon real vanilla extract if you did not use vanilla beans and whisk. Pour into a glass pitcher, cover mixture and refrigerate 6 hours or until 38 degrees. Be sure you have a thermometer in your refrigerator and keep it between 34-38 degrees-over 40 degrees is optimal temperature for bacterial growth!

Follow the manufacturer's ice cream machine instructions to churn. When finished churning, pour into plastic containers and freeze for 8 hours or overnight for premium ice cream texture, or eat a little of it now, which will be soft serve consistency. Scoop and enjoy!

*Note: you can use all light coconut milk, but the texture will not be as creamy.

Vanilla Cupcakes

Cupcakes are a popular favorite for everyone! Great for traveling or when you want an individual dessert neatly wrapped in its own packaging. Kids love this at parties! Adults can eat this small portion with much less guilt than a large piece of cake!

Yields: 24 cupcakes, regular size

3 ½ cups oat flour

2 teaspoons baking soda

2 teaspoons baking powder

1 teaspoon sea salt, fine

¼ cup grapeseed oil

2/3 cup agave nectar

2 cups coconut milk or unsweetened almond milk

2 teaspoons apple cider vinegar

1 Tablespoon real vanilla extract or 2 vanilla beans

Preheat oven to 350 degrees. Oil pan with vegan Earth Balance or grapeseed oil or place paper liners into cups. Sift all dry ingredients into the bowl of an electric stand mixer. Measure out all liquid ingredients and add to dry ingredients. If using vanilla beans, cut in half lengthwise and scrape out seeds with the back of a knife. Whisk the vanilla bean into the wet ingredients. Place paddle attachment onto mixer and mix on low speed just until incorporated. Stop mixer and scrape down sides and bottom of the bowl, mix briefly until smooth. Pour batter into cupcake pan or liners filling ¾ of the way to the top. Place muffin pan on a baking sheet. Bake on the middle rack of oven for 20 minutes. Insert a toothpick in the middle of the cupcake and it is done when it comes out clean. If it does not come out clean continue baking approximately 5 more minutes. Cool on a rack until completely cool. Frost with "buttercream" or Ganache. Decorate with fresh berries or whatever you like.

For transporting place cupcakes back into a clean cupcake pan. Insert a toothpick into all four cupcakes in each corner and one in the center so they are sticking up ¾ of the way out the top. Gently cover with foil, put into a large shopping bag with handles and place on the floor of your car and take it slowly around those corners! Trust me on the driving tip!

Vanilla Pudding

This is so creamy that you will never miss the cream! Your friends will think that it is the traditional version, and you will convert them! I like to serve it and after hearing all the accolades, announce the ingredients! People are very pleasantly surprised!

2 cups organic coconut milk, regular

1 vanilla bean* or 1 Tablespoon real vanilla extract

6 lg. egg yolks

1/3 cup agave nectar

¼ cup tapioca starch** or cornstarch

1 teaspoon real vanilla extract

1 Tablespoon vegan Earth Balance, optional

In a 2 quart saucepot, bring the coconut milk and vanilla bean to a boil-watch it closely. Set aside and cool for about 10 minutes while getting all your ingredients together. If you are using real vanilla extract instead of the vanilla bean, which I don't recommend, just heat the coconut milk and reserve the extract for the end. In an electric stand mixer, with the whisk attachment, on medium-high speed whisk egg yolks and agave until fluffy-about 5 minutes. Turn off mixer and add tapioca starch and mix on low until there are no lumps. Scrape down bowl and mix until incorporated. On low speed add ¼ cup warm coconut milk to egg mixture. Add the egg mixture to the coconut milk in the saucepot. Cook mixture over low heat whisking constantly-scraping the bottom and sides just until thick. Do not let this boil or over cook or it will scramble the eggs. You can put this into a double boiler instead of cooking directly over the heat, it will just take longer, but won't scramble. Whisk in real vanilla extract. Remove from heat and whisk in the vegan Earth Balance if desired, which will make is more glossy. Pour into a glass dish or ceramic ramekins. Cover with plastic wrap so it is touching the top of the pudding to prevent a skin from forming. Chill in refrigerator for at least 3 hours or longer. Top with fresh fruit or berries.

*It is well worth using the vanilla bean for more flavor and texture.

** Tapioca starch has a sweeter and nicer flavor than cornstarch without the chalkiness. Cornstarch is fine. However, many people are sensitive to corn.

Vegan Chocolate Chip Cookies

Enjoy theses classic chocolate chip cookies without any animal ingredients! Place a scoop of Ice "Cream" in between two cookies for a wonderful vegan dessert!

Yields: 24 cookies

¼ cup grapeseed oil

¾ cup pure maple syrup or agave nectar

1 tsp. real vanilla extract

2 cups oat flour

½ teaspoon baking soda

½ teaspoon baking powder

½ teaspoon sea salt, finely ground

1 cup chocolate chips, non-dairy

½ cup chopped walnuts, optional

Preheat oven to 350 degrees. In an electric stand mixer, with the paddle attachment, combine oil, maple syrup or agave and real vanilla extract. Sift together all dry ingredients into a bowl, add to the wet ingredients in electric mixer and mix on low speed just until combined. Stir in chocolate chips and nuts. Refrigerate dough for 1 hour. Dip a 1 Tablespoon ice cream scooper or measuring spoon into cookie dough and place them onto a cookie sheet. Use a cup of very hot water to dip the scooper in between cookies so dough does not stick. Bake for 12 minutes. Remove from oven and let cool for 5 minutes on the baking sheet, then remove cookies from pan with a spatula onto a wire cooling rack. Enjoy. These make great ice "cream" sandwiches-see index for recipes!

Many of the recipes in this cookbook are vegan, read and enjoy!

Yellow Cake

A moist and delicious cake that can be transformed into many variations. Since this uses agave as the sweetener the glycemic index is very low and will not have the same effect as refined sugar. Makes the perfect children's birthday cake!

Yields: 1 (9x13) cake or two 8 inch round cakes

3 ½ cups oat flour

2 teaspoons baking soda

2 teaspoons baking powder

1 teaspoon sea salt, fine

¼ cup grapeseed oil

2/3 cup agave nectar

2 cups coconut milk or unsweetened almond milk*

2 teaspoons apple cider vinegar

1 Tablespoon real vanilla extract or 2 vanilla beans

Preheat oven to 350 degrees. Oil pan with vegan Earth Balance or grapeseed oil, then dust with oat flour and tap out any excess. Sift all dry ingredients into the bowl of an electric stand mixer or a bowl and use an electric hand mixer. Measure out all liquid ingredients and add to dry ingredients. If using vanilla beans, cut in half lengthwise and scrape out seeds with the back of a knife. Whisk the vanilla bean seeds into the wet ingredients. Put vanilla pod into a bag of sucanat or maple sugar to flavor. Place paddle attachment onto mixer and mix on low speed just until incorporated. Stop mixer and scrape down sides and bottom of the bowl, mix briefly just until combined- over mixing will make the cake tough. Pour batter into cake pan and bake on the middle rack of oven for 40 minutes. Insert a toothpick in the middle of the cake and it is done when it comes out clean. If it does not come out clean continue baking approximately 5 more minutes or until toothpick comes out clean. Cool on a wire rack until completely cool. Remove from round pans. You can keep it in the 9x13 pan. Frost with "Buttercream" or Chocolate Ganache (see index). This unfrosted cake can be double wrapped in plastic and then put into a freezer plastic zip bag and frozen for up to one month.

*unsweetened rice or soy milk may be substituted

Dairy Names

The word "dairy" when used as an adjective generally means "made from milk". Caseins and sodium caseinate are milk derivatives. It is misleading to claim a product is "non dairy" or "dairy-free" when it contains a milk ingredient or derivative or made from these ingredients. The following are some examples of milk ingredients and derivatives:

butter, butter oil, milk fat
caseinate (ammonium/calcium/magnesium/
    potassium/sodium)
casein/rennet casein
hydrolyzed casein, hydrolyzed milk protein
cheese, cheese curds
lactalbumin/lactalbumin phosphate
lactoferrin
lactoglobulin
lactate (when made from milk ingredients)
lactitol
lactose
milk, skimmed milk, partially skimmed milk, cream,
    buttermilk
sour cream, sour milk solids
whey, whey butter, whey cream , whey protein con-
    centrate
delactosed/demineralized whey

Simplesse® (whey protein concentrate-micropartic-
ulated fat replacers)
yogurt

When a claim is made that a product is "free" from
a substance or that it is not present in a food, the
substance must not be added directly or indirectly
as an ingredient component to a food.

Wheat Names

The following ingredients found on a label indicate the presence of wheat protein. All labels should be read carefully before consuming a product.

All purpose flour
Bran
Bread (any type made with white flour, wheat flour), bread crumbs
Bread flour
Bromated flour
Bulgur
Cake flour
Cereal extract
Club wheat (Triticum compactum Host.)
Common wheat (Triticum aestivum L.)
Couscous
Crackers, cracker meal
Durum wheat (Triticum durum Desf.)
Durum flour
Einkorn (Triticum monococcum L. subsp. monococcum)
Emmer (Triticum turgidum L. subsp. dicoccon (Schrank) Thell.)
Enriched flour
Farina
Flour
Fu

Germ

Gluten

Graham flour

High gluten flour

High protein flour

Instant flour

Kamut (Triticum polonicum L.)

Malt, malt extract

Matzo, Matzoh, Matzah, Matza, matsa, matso

Matzo meal, Matzoh meal, Matzah meal, Matza meal ,matsa meal, matso meal, matsah meal or matsoh meal

Noodles

Pasta

Pastry flour

Phosphated flour

Plain flour

Seitan

Self-rising flour

Semolina (Triticum durum Desf.)

Soft wheat flour

Spelt (Triticum spelta L.)

Steel ground flour

Stone ground flour

Tabbouleh

Triticale (x Triticosecale ssp. Wittm.)

Triticum: Triticum aestivum L., Triticum durum Desf., Triticum compactum Host., Triticum spelta L., Triticum durum Desf., Triticum monococcum L. subsp. monococcum, Triticum turgidum L. subsp. dicoc-

con (Schrank) Thell., Triticum polonicum L., and x
Triticosecale ssp. Wittm.

Unbleached flour

Vital gluten

Wheat, wheat berries, wheat bran, wheat flour,
wheat germ, wheat gluten, wheat grass, wheat
malt, wheat starch, wheat sprouts

White flour

Whole wheat berries

Whole wheat bread

Whole wheat flour

May indicate the presence of wheat:

Artificial flavoring

Caramel color

Dextrin

Food starch*

Gelatinized starch*

Hydrolyzed vegetable protein (HVP)

Maltodextrin

Modified food starch*

Monosodium glutamate

MSG

Natural flavoring

Shoyu

Soy Sauce

Surimi

Tamari

Teriyaki Sauce

Textured vegetable protein
Vegetable gum
Vegetable starch*

Kitchen Equipment

Electric Stand Mixer-Heavy Duty is best. I like Kitchen Aid with paddle, whisk, dough hook, and freezer ice cream bowl attachments. You can use an electric hand mixer instead.

Food Processor-large sized is best. I like Cuisinart.

Blender-stand and hand blenders are great. Vita mixers are the best, but very expensive.

Kitchen Timer

Oven Thermometer

Meat/Food Thermometer AND Candy Thermometer-reads over 250 degrees

Whisks-tiny, small and large

Silicone or Rubber Spatula and Wooden Spoon

Chef's Knife-8 inch, Paring Knife

Cutting Boards-Bamboo is best, Wood, Plastic color coded. Do not use glass.

Glass Measuring Cups-2 cup and 4 cup for liquid ingredients

Metal or Plastic Measuring Cups-for dry ingredients

Measuring Spoons

Microplane Zester/Grater

Sauce Pots-2 quart and soup pot

Sauté Pan-12 inch Stainless Steel, and Cast Iron

Glass Baking Pans- 9x13, 8x8, 2 loaf pans

Stainless Steel Cake Pans- 2 round (8-10 inches)

Stainless Steel Baking Sheet Pans

Metal or Glass Mixing Bowls

Kitchen Aid Ice Cream Freezer Bowl attachment or Ice Cream Maker.

Wire cooling Rack-for cookies

Fine mesh strainer- to strain sauces, puddings, and can be used as a sifter for dry ingredients

Stainless Steel Ice Cream Scooper

Glass Jar-shake thickener and water together to make a "slurry"

Pot holders-cotton and silicone (good to place under a mixing bowl to keep from sliding)

Resources

JonesandBones.com

(831) 462-0521

Specialty olive oils, citrus olive oils/vinegars, spices, exotic salts/peppers, varietal honey, vanilla/extracts, chocolate, kitchen equipment/accessories, lots of unique gourmet items and gifts that they will carefully pack and ship to your home! Exceptional customer service too!

Trader Joe's

agave nectar, light coconut milk, almond milk, rice milk, soy milk, real maple syrup, chocolate, produce, meat, organic wine, oils, nuts, oats, vegan Earth Balance, stock/broth

Whole Foods Market

flours, vegan Earth Balance sticks/spread, tapioca starch, Eggology egg whites, almond paste, Valrhona cocoa powder, agave nectar, regular and light coconut milk, almond milk, rice milk, soy milk, real maple syrup/maple sugar, date sugar, sucanat, chocolate, produce, meat, organic wine, oils, nuts, oats, stock/broth

Buffalo and other Meat etc... Buffalo and Meat information and purchasing sources:

www.agricultureb2b.com/biz/e/Farm-Products/Fresh-Meats/5.htm

bobsredmill.com- many grain flours (oat, barley, quinoa, amaranth, rye, millet etc...)

(800) 349-2173

arrowheadmills.com- many grain flours (oat, barley, quinoa, blue cornmeal etc...)

(800) 858.4308

bluediamond.com- almond milk

pacificfoods.com- almond milk, rice milk, soy milk, chicken and vegetable stock

503-692-9666

dagobachocolate.com- chocolate

(866) 608-6944

sunspire.com- dairy-free, gluten-free, vegan chocolate chips.

(510) 569-9731

williams-sonoma.com- kitchen equipment

I always like to support local small businesses and farmers, so go and see what is available there first. There are lots of great farmers markets you can visit or they will deliver to your home.

Helpful Websites and Articles

Coconut Milk/Oil information:
http://www.westonaprice.org/
knowyourfats/coconut-oil-studies.html
http://www.aja.org.br/oleos-/coconut_oil_good_
saturated_fat.pdf

Food Allergy and Anaphylaxis Network: www.
foodallergy.org
www.kidswithfoodallergies.org

Buffalo and Meat information and purchasing
sources:
www.agricultureb2b.com/biz/e/Farm-Products/
Fresh-Meats/5.htm

Body care and organic helpful tips/blog
www.idealbite.org

Bibliography

Garten, Ina. *Barefoot Contessa Back to Basics/ Parties*. New York, Clarkson Potter/Publishers 2008.

Leader, Daniel. *Bread Alone*. New York. William Morrow and Company, Inc. 1993.

Niall, Mani. *Covered in Honey*. Rodale. 2003.

Kaimal-MacMillan, Maya. *Curried Flavors*. New York. Abbeville Press. 1996.

Torres, Jacques. *Dessert Circus*. New York. William Morrow and Company, Inc. 1998.

Luchetti, Emily. *Four-Star Desserts*. New York. Harper Collins Publishers, Inc. 1996.

Engelhart, Terces with Orchid. *I Am Grateful*. Berkeley, California. North Atlantic Books. 2007.

Beard, James and Jerome, Carl. *New Recipes for the Cuisinart*. Cuisinart inc. 1976 and 1978.

Prudhomme, Paul. *Chef Paul Prudhomme's Louisiana Kitchen*. New York. William Morrow and Company, Inc. 1984.

Chase, Sarah Leah. *Pedaling Through Provence Cookbook*. Workman Publishing Company. 1995.

Jardine, Denise. *Recipes for Dairy-Free Living*. Berkeley, California. Celestial Arts. 2001.

Abraham, Ellen. *Simple Treats*. Summertown, Tennessee. Book Publishing Company. 2003.

Index

W

Y

Z

About the Author

Graduating from the California Culinary Academy Lauren embarked on a culinary career which led her to being a Pastry Chef. Some of the places she worked include: La Folie Restaurant, Hyatt Resorts, Marriott Resorts, Fairmont Hotel, Bally's Hotel and Casino, Wente Brother's Winery, San Francisco Chronicle and Veggie Life Magazine. She went onto teach culinary school in California after working on the East Coast and Switzerland. She returned to college to earn a Psychology degree.

Lauren developed food allergies and converted, created and tested recipes without wheat, dairy and refined sugar using familiar, healthy ingredients including: Coconut/ Almond Milk, Oat Flour, Grapeseed/Olive Oils, vegan Earth Balance, Agave and Maple Syrup, and offers alternatives for these ingredients.

Recipes include: Chili, Meatballs, Bourguignon, Stroganoff, Meatloaf, Mashed Potatoes, Cream Sauce, Pot Pie, Fried Chicken, and many desserts including: Pudding, Ice Cream, Cakes, Cheesecake, Buttercream, Cookies, Cream Puffs and Chocolate Truffles! In addition, a few of her favorite recipes such as: Lemonade, Sautéed Rainbow Chard, Roasted Carrots and Parsnips, Hummus and Raspberry Sauce. Some delicious Vegan recipes included are: Breads,

Mushroom Pot Pie, Vegetables, Beverages, Cakes, Cookies, Pies and more!

Her writing style has clear directions and is educational, beyond cooking, with glimpses into her personality and life. Inspired recipes from her family to famous chefs, helpful hints, ingredient information, resources and websites including her own blog site all contribute to a valuable resource for everyone with food allergies, sensitivities, limited diets and everyone else who is seeking something new!

Cover Photographs

Front Cover from Top Left to Bottom Left: Vanilla Ice Cream Sundae with Chocolate Ganache, Lemon Tart, Fried Chicken and Mashed Potatoes.

Front Cover from Top Right to Bottom Right: Brownies, Vanilla Pudding, Tempura.

Back Cover from Top Left to Bottom Left: Pancakes, Chocolate Cake with Ganache, Pumpkin Cheesecake with Ginger Cookie Crust.

Back Cover from Top Right to Bottom Right: Blueberry Crisp, Scones with Lemon Curd, Assorted Cookies.